BOMB AIMER
OVER
BERLIN

BOMB AIMER

OVER

BERLIN

*The Wartime Memoirs of
Les Bartlett* DFM

by

Peter Jacobs
with
Les Bartlett

Pen & Sword
AVIATION

First published in Great Britain in 2007 by
Pen & Sword Aviation
an imprint of
Pen & Sword Books Ltd

Copyright © Peter Jacobs 2007

ISBN 978-1-84415-596-5

British Library Cataloguing-in-Publication Data
A CIP catalogue record for this book is
available from the British Library

Typeset in Palatino by
Phoenix Typesetting, Auldgirth, Dumfriesshire

Printed and bound in England by
Biddles Ltd, King's Lynn

Pen & Sword Books Ltd incorporates the Imprints of Pen & Sword Aviation,
Pen & Sword Maritime, Pen & Sword Military, Wharncliffe Local History,
Pen & Sword Select, Pen & Sword Military Classics and Leo Cooper.

For a complete list of Pen & Sword titles please contact
PEN & SWORD BOOKS LIMITED
47 Church Street, Barnsley, South Yorkshire, S70 2AS, England
E-mail: enquiries@pen-and-sword.co.uk
Website: www.pen-and-sword.co.uk

To Les Bartlett DFM and all the other brave men
who served with Bomber Command during
the Second World War.

Acknowledgements

First and foremost I would like to thank Les Bartlett, the main subject of this book, for allowing me access to his diary and material over so many years. Without his co-operation and that of others, authors such as myself would not be able to pass on the stories and experiences of the gallant men of Bomber Command during the Second World War. I must also thank the two other surviving members of Les's wartime crew, Reg Payne and Sir Michael Beetham. Reg, in particular, has proved to be an excellent second source of information and has always provided me with material and information in a most timely manner.

There are many other former members of Bomber Command, far too many to mention them all, who have helped me with their stories and photographs over the years; my thanks to them all. I would also like to thank the staff at the Air Historical Branch at Bentley Priory, in particular Graham Day and Mary Hudson for their help and cooperation over so many years. Finally from my side, I would like to thank Peter Coles at Pen & Sword. I know how much this book means to Les and without Peter's full support it would not have been possible.

Both Les and I would like to thank Martin Middlebrook and Chris Everitt for allowing the use of facts and figures from their excellent reference work *Bomber Command War Diaries*; if anyone is not familiar with this work, I fully commend it to you. Les would also like me to record his thanks to Dahlia Hill for typing his diary, Mark Chisnell, Patsy Ledger and Charlie Campbell of the Southampton Branch of the Air Crew Association for their continual encouragement over the years, and David Dowdell, who was Les's guiding light with computers. Finally, Les would also like me to record his thanks to his daughter Christine, and to his late wife, Margaret, who always insisted that he should not throw away his diary but sadly died before she could see his story told.

Foreword

I was still at Stockton Secondary School when a friend of mine told me that some aeroplanes had arrived at nearby Thornaby airfield over the weekend. That was enough for me. On the following Saturday morning I jumped on my bike and rode the 6 miles in record time. I found a hole in the hedge and got a glimpse of the Westland Wapitis of No. 608 (North Riding) Auxiliary Air Force; they were beautiful. It was June 1930 and I was still only twelve years old, but my mind was made up and the Royal Air Force would be the life for me.

Sixteen years later I returned to Thornaby once more. By then I was a flight lieutenant and was coming to the end of my time in the RAF. I was soon to be demobbed but I thoroughly enjoyed my short time back at the airfield where, for me, it had all begun. Much had happened to me in those sixteen years, some of which I would never forget. Although my five years in the RAF did not particularly change the overall pattern of my life (I was in pharmacy before I joined up and returned to my profession at the end of the war), my time in Bomber Command certainly changed my outlook and the memories of my tour of operations during the winter of 1943/4 remain unforgettable. There was never an easy time to complete a tour of operations but that particular winter was a hard one and the Battle of Berlin was a difficult campaign. Ten of my operational sorties were flown against the 'Big City' and the name 'Berlin' became part of my life.

Anyone who survived a tour of operations with Bomber Command will appreciate how lucky we were. The odds were not good, as the list of more than 55,000 men killed or missing confirms. Now, more than sixty years after the end of the Second World War, I am glad that I had the presence of mind to record the events of my life during those difficult years. More recently, I always wondered whether I would get the chance to tell my story; not because I wanted people to know about me but because I wanted people to understand what it was like to serve in Bomber Command during the war. However, after too many unsuccessful attempts I felt about ready to give up. Then my close friend Peter Jacobs offered to help and here we are with this book, and I am so grateful to Peter and to the publishers Pen & Sword for telling this story.

Contents

Introduction

Les Bartlett's wartime experience, and indeed his life, would have been so different had he stayed in the world of pharmacy. Having qualified as a pharmacist soon after the outbreak of the Second World War, he was in a reserved occupation and exempt from military duty. The idea behind reserved occupations was that certain jobs and skills across the country were considered too valuable to the overall war effort and a male workforce was held back rather than being called forward for service in the armed forces. However, the increasing number of casualties as the war progressed soon led to the situation being reviewed. By the end of 1940 more than 5 million women were in employment all across Britain. Whilst most of these were employed in occupations such as factory work, working on the land or driving vehicles, the precedent had been set and the door opened for Les. Like many young men, he was keen to join up and 'do his bit for King and Country' and so he volunteered for service as aircrew in the Royal Air Force during 1941.

Les completed his tour of operations as a bomb aimer with No. 50 Sqn Bomber Command during the long, hard winter of 1943/4. Based at RAF Skellingthorpe near Lincoln, he began his tour as a sergeant and ended it as a pilot officer, having been awarded the Distinguished Flying Medal for gallantry along the way. Ten of his operational sorties were flown against Berlin during the bombing offensive that later became known as the Battle of Berlin.

Statistically there was never an easy time to do a tour of operations with Bomber Command. Its offensive against Germany lasted from the opening day of the Second World War and continued without rest until the end of the war in Europe. During that time Bomber Command lost over 55,000 men dead, the majority of whom were killed on operations; taking the number of wounded and prisoners of war into account, the total number of Bomber Command casualties was nearly 74,000. This is extremely high when one considers that 125,000 aircrew served in Bomber Command during the Second World War; in other words, each individual faced a 40 per cent probability that he would be killed or a 60 per cent probability that he would be killed, wounded or taken as a prisoner of war.

Les was one of the 40 per cent who survived unscathed, apart from having memories of those who were not so lucky, and after the war he returned to pharmacy, the profession he had left when he volunteered for active service. By contrast his pilot, Mike Beetham, stayed in the post-war RAF and went on to become Marshal of the Royal Air Force Sir Michael Beetham GCB CBE DFC AFC.

I had a chance meeting with Les one Sunday morning in June 1989. At the time I was a flight lieutenant navigator instructor at Finningley. Having finished a tour on the Phantom at Coningsby, I had bought a house on a residential estate in Lincoln as it was likely that I would soon return to Coningsby and Lincoln was mid-way between the two stations. I was in my car and on my way to buy a newspaper at the local newsagent when the Lancaster 'City of Lincoln' from the Battle of Britain Memorial Flight passed directly overhead at 'flypast height'. A few moments later I noticed that the road ahead was closed and there were many people gathered around talking. I parked the car and strolled down to take a closer look at what was going on. Amongst the gathering I noticed a number of men proudly wearing their medals and admiring a most impressive memorial.

I knew a bit about medals and approached one wearing the

Distinguished Flying Medal; it turned out to be Les. So began
a long friendship, which has lasted to this day. Les and I have
so much in common; not only do we both understand flying
in the RAF, albeit in somewhat different circumstances, but
Les lives close to my home near Southampton. From my
conversations with him during those first meetings, I soon
learned what the memorial was all about and about the existence of the Nos 50 and 61 Squadrons Association. I also
learned that my house was on the former site of RAF
Skellingthorpe, from which both squadrons had operated
Lancasters during the Second World War.

I found myself becoming more and more fascinated by the
whole story. Les had been on the Association's Memorial
Committee and he explained to me that there were plans to
produce a Roll of Honour and that the Association was about
to pay a large sum of money to a professional historian to
complete the work. As I had an interest in RAF history, and
this was all happening at a time when I was just beginning to
get started in writing, I offered to do the work for nothing
apart from the expenses incurred travelling to and from the
Air Historical Branch in London.

The Roll of Honour, which includes the names of 1,976
aircrew and ground personnel killed whilst serving with the
two squadrons during the Second World War, was dedicated
at a service held at the memorial in 1991. By then I had got to
know Les well and had written other articles on him and his
crew. The reason I was able to do this was because Les had
provided me with much original material that he had kept
from during the war, including his diary from his tour of
operations. Despite wartime restrictions, Les had had the
presence of mind to record his experiences as they were
happening at the time, and it was apparent to me how special
his diary was.

Incidentally, my interest in RAF Skellingthorpe and its two
wartime squadrons increased as I got to know more of those
who flew from the airfield during the Second World War.
Although there is a long-standing saying in the military,

'never volunteer for anything', my initial passing interest in the Association led to me eventually becoming its Chairman, something, I consider to be an honour and a privilege. Furthermore, I get a great deal of pleasure seeing Les back with the two other surviving members of his wartime crew, Sir Michael Beetham and Reg Payne, at the Association's annual reunion at the former site of RAF Skellingthorpe.

Throughout the last few years it has become increasingly obvious to me that Les's story should be told; not because it is particularly different from those of others serving in Bomber Command at the time, but because his diary represents what all those young men went through during the difficult period of the Battle of Berlin in the winter of 1943/4. Therefore, it is Les's diary that forms the basis of this book.

At the time of writing, Les is approaching his ninetieth birthday. My family has welcomed him into our home so many times over the past eighteen years and we have all got to know him so well. Indeed, it has been an education for my children to learn about what happened during the Second World War on the site where we now live. Les Bartlett is a remarkable man with a remarkable story. Enjoy the book!

CHAPTER ONE

A Willing Volunteer

The son of an engineer, Les Bartlett might well have been born in Russia. His father, Albert Bartlett, had been working for the Tsarist Government since 1913, and had helped establish a canning factory in the Omsk region of Siberia. His work in Russia proved successful and so the Government, keen to retain his services, paid for his girl-friend, Beatrice Rudge, to travel out from her home in Gloucester to join him and the couple were married in the Evangelical-Lutheran Church in Omsk on 12 January 1915. Having previously lost a baby daughter after just four months, the couple decided to take no chances second time around and Beatrice returned to Gloucester, where she gave birth to Albert Leslie Bartlett on 17 September 1917. By then the Russian Revolution was gathering momentum and so his father left Russia soon after to rejoin the family in Gloucester, although he had to leave his wealth behind in Russia.

Sadly, Les's father died of pneumonia in 1919 having never recovered from rescuing a woman who had fallen into the River Severn. His mother bought a small newsagent and confectionery business in Gloucester to make ends meet. For the next few years Les grew up in Gloucestershire. On his sixth birthday he came across the word 'Berlin' for the first time. Amongst the presents he received for his birthday, one aroused his curiosity more than the others. It was a shallow wooden box about 8 inches by 6 inches and about 1 inch deep. The top was a sheet of glass through which he could see inside. There was a winding channel cut into the inside of the base, which meandered from side to side starting at the bottom left-hand corner and eventually ending at the top right-hand corner. The idea was to negotiate a ballbearing past a number of holes in the channel in order to get it to the top of the game. Beside each hole there was the name of a city. It was a German toy and therefore all the cities were in Germany. The aim of the game was to get the ballbearing up to the top hole called 'Berlin'. Not surprisingly, being only six years old, that was the first time Les had heard of Berlin and he could never have imagined the significance it would have later in his life, although he never forgot that first encounter.

A few years later his mother met and eventually married a ship's engineer called Hornsey Gamlen. The family moved north-east to where the ship-building companies were located and initially settled in Hartlepool in 1927 before moving to Billingham, near Stockton-on-Tees, a year later. They settled in Roseberry Road, Billingham, but the next few years do not have fond memories for Les. His half-brother, Fred, was born in 1927 and Les found himself feeling very much like excess baggage; in his own words, he could not wait to get away.

Aeroplanes had first caught his eye as a young boy during the 1920s, when he noticed them on the back page of the *Daily Express*. He sent away for a glider, which he paid for with his pocket money, and cut out the pictures from the newspaper and spread them across his bedroom wall, much to the annoyance of his mother. Photographs in daily newspapers were not the only influence on the young Les Bartlett. Pictures of aeroplanes on the billboards at the entrance to the local Billingham Picture House promoting Howard Hughes's 1930 film about pilots in the First World War called *Hell's Angels*, which starred Ben Lyon and James Hall and featured a starring debut by a young Jean Harlow, led to Les seeing the film three times during the following week! It had been the most expensive film to make at that time and included some spectacular flying sequences, but what Les would not have known then, and it might well have put a thirteen-year-old boy off, was that three pilots had been killed during the making of the film; such were the hazards of aviation at the time.

Like many young boys, pictures in newspapers or films of aeroplanes were never going to be enough for him. In March 1930, No. 608 (North Riding) Sqn formed at nearby Thornaby airfield as an Auxiliary Air Force day-bomber unit. The site had been used as a second class landing ground during the First World War and was developed during the late 1920s. Although the airfield had very few facilities, the squadron's Westland Wapitis began to arrive in June 1930. This, understandably, created much interest in the local area. Although the airfield was 6 miles away from his home, the bike ride was well worth it and Les's mind was made up, it simply had to be the RAF.

At the time Les was studying at Stockton Secondary School for Boys and it was to be three more years before he was able to take his desire to join the RAF one step further. At sixteen years old he saw an advertisement in the local paper – 'Examinations will be held for boy entrants into the RAF at Stockton Town Hall.' This was his chance to join the RAF and he sat the examination. On 29 December 1933 he received a brown envelope containing a letter to say that he had passed the examination and enclosing a travel warrant to RAF Halton. In the early period after the First World War, aircraft maintenance was becoming increasingly technical and the RAF needed to train a number of personnel in a wide variety of trades. Lord Trenchard had developed the idea of a Boy Mechanics Training School, which had been set up at Halton in 1917 to produce riggers for the Royal Flying Corps and was renamed No.1 School of Technical Training in 1920. Halton received its first entry of boys in January 1922 and the rank of aircraft apprentice was adopted. During the 1920s each entry was typically 500 strong but by the early 1930s this had reduced by half. However, from 1934 the numbers steadily increased as the RAF expanded with the increasing instability in Europe.

It was against this background that Les arrived at Halton a few days later; he was delighted. However, his elation was not to last long and his enthusiasm for the RAF disappeared almost immediately; two weeks after his arrival he was on his way home again! His short experience of 'bossy corporals', whitewashing stones, polishing lino and continual drill were more than sixteen-year-old Bartlett could take. His commanding officer gave him a progress report at the end of the second week. Contrary to what might normally have been expected of a young recruit, Les decided to make his own views known and took the opportunity to give the commanding officer the benefit of his opinion. Seen as a potential trouble maker and a bad influence on the rest of his flight, he was on his way back to the north-east with a one-way travel warrant in his hand; it was probably the best outcome at the time for both Les and the RAF!

It was still only mid-January 1934 when Les arrived back home and he went back to school in time to start the spring term, with his brief experience of the RAF behind him. Interestingly, he kept quiet about the Halton episode when he later volunteered again for the RAF in 1941; he did not want to spoil his chances next time round.

For the next five years Les put his sojourn with the RAF well and truly behind him as he concentrated on making a career in pharmacy. He served a three-year apprenticeship at Levi Chemist in Stockton-on-Tees, which he completed in 1937. It was also in 1937 that he met Margaret Gowland, who lived in the same road. Although it was early days, the couple's friendship quickly blossomed.

Les then attended the School of Pharmacy at Sunderland Technical College, as he prepared for his final pharmacy examinations, Britain was preparing for war. The outbreak of hostilities on 3 September 1939 caused his final examinations, due to be held in London, to be postponed. Instead, he had to go north to Edinburgh in January to sit them. On 20 February 1940, he received confirmation that he had passed his finals and was from that moment a qualified chemist and druggist, and a member of the Pharmaceutical Society.

As a pharmacist Les was in a reserved occupation, which prevented him from joining the armed forces. However, he wanted to 'do his bit' and so joined the Air Raid Precautions (ARP) as an ambulance driver. The ARP was dedicated to the protection of civilians from the danger of air raids. It had been created in 1924 as a response to the increasing threat of long-range bomber aircraft, and during the Second World War was responsible for the upkeep of local air-raid shelters, handing out gas masks, maintenance of the 'blackout' and rescuing people following air raids. Les served with the ARP during the summer of 1940, and when not on duty he was the locum for the local pharmacist, who also happened to be Commandant of the first-aid post.

The war came to the north-east of England at lunch time on 15 August 1940. With the exception of those who had friends or family involved in the fighting across the Channel in France or in the southern counties during the opening weeks of what later became known as the Battle of Britain, this was the first occasion that many of the civilians in the north-east experienced the reality of war.

Seventy Heinkel He111s escorted by twenty Messerschmitt Bf110s of *Luftflotte 5* had taken off from Stavanger in Norway to attack airfields of No. 13 Group and industrial targets in the Tyne-Tees area; a further fifty Junkers Ju88s had taken off from Aalborg in Denmark to attack airfields of No. 12 Group in Yorkshire. The decision by the *Luftwaffe* to attack targets so far north was unexpected and came as a complete surprise to the RAF squadrons given the task of defending the north of England and Scotland. Up until then the *Luftwaffe*'s raids had generally been concentrated in the south-east, although some had ventured as far north as the Midlands, Merseyside and Leeds, but none as far as the north-east. For the *Luftwaffe*, any assumption that the RAF's fighters were all in the south proved costly and the Spitfires of No. 616 Sqn (Leconfield), No. 41 Sqn (Catterick) and No. 72 Sqn (Acklington), and Hurricanes of No. 79 Sqn (Acklington), No. 605 Sqn (Drem) and No. 73 Sqn (Church Fenton) enjoyed great success. In the raid against the north-east, three of the escorting Messerschmitts were shot down and the rest fled for the cover of cloud, leaving the unescorted Heinkels to fend for themselves and scatter their bombs over the Sunderland-Newcastle area. Fortunately, because of the range, each bomber's load had been reduced to 3,000lb per aircraft and the scattered bombing resulted in little damage of any significance.

The RAF did not suffer any losses during the air fighting but there was considerable damage to the Bomber Command airfield at Driffield, including twelve aircraft destroyed on the ground and thirteen personnel killed. In addition to the three Bf110s shot down, the *Luftwaffe* lost eight He111s from KG26 and seven Ju88s of KG30 during the raids in the north and north-east. Two of the Heinkels came down in the Middlesbrough area but both crashed into the sea and no bombs fell where Les had been during the raids. It had, therefore, been a normal day for him but it was a sharp reminder to everyone in the north-east that the nation was at war. However, it was also a bad day for *Luftflotte* 5 and the losses suffered meant that it would play no further part in the Battle of Britain.

The review of government policy regarding reserved occupations gave many young men the chance to join up. Les's opportunity came early in 1941 when he answered the nation's appeal for aircrew and he went straight to the recruiting office in Middlesbrough to offer his services as a pilot in the RAF Volunteer Reserve. The RAF's expansion plans of the mid-1930s had called for a larger number of pilots than could be supplied by the regular recruiting and training resources at the time. Whilst the Auxiliary Air Force (AAF) had been in existence since 1924, it was not deemed to be the right organization for what the RAF had in mind. First, although the AAF pilots were volunteers, they were all commissioned and of a certain social standing; the annual cost to an individual was typically in the order of £50 per year, which was not readily affordable for most young men, no matter how keen they were or how capable they might have been as pilots. Secondly, the organization of the AAF was very regional: squadrons were formed on a city or county basis. And so the RAF Volunteer Reserve was formed in January 1937, the idea being to attract and recruit young men from a wide social background, and from all educational backgrounds.

One significant difference between the RAFVR and AAF was the rank structure of its members. Whilst AAF pilots were commissioned officers, volunteers for the RAFVR were attested in the rank of aircraftman second class (AC2) followed by instant promotion to sergeant the following day. Those who subsequently proved worthy of commissioning were further promoted. Flying training was conducted along very similar lines to the AAF, during evenings or at weekends, or at short summer camps. Each reservist was expected to fly a total of about sixty hours per year and flying training was carried out on various aircraft such as the Tiger Moth, Hawker Hind and Miles Magister. However, unlike the AAF, the RAFVR was not organized into squadrons; ground training was carried out in towns and cities across the country but generally close to airfields where the flying training took place.

Whilst early volunteers might well have seen the RAFVR as an opportunity to learn to fly, the threat of war with Germany saw a rise in patriotism and an increasing number of volunteers. By the outbreak of the Second World War there were about 5,000 RAFVR pilots. Their contribution to the war effort proved to be immediate and immense. Of nearly 2,500 pilots and more than 500 other aircrew who flew during the Battle of Britain, one-third were members of the Volunteer Reserve.

The RAFVR was, quite simply, just what Les was looking for. Within days of volunteering he received his notice paper to report to No. 3 Recruits Centre at RAF Padgate near Warrington, Lancashire, where he would be enlisted into the RAFVR on 1 May 1941. The notice paper was quite clear and to the point. He was a volunteer for the 'duration of the present emergency' and it laid out the eight general conditions of the Contract of Enlistment that Les was about to enter into with the Crown, which were as follows:

1. You will engage to serve His Majesty as an airman for the duration of the present Emergency, provided His Majesty should so long require your services.

2. On enlistment into the Royal Air Force Volunteer Reserve, you will be liable, if medically fit, to carry out duty in the air in any type of aircraft and may be ordered to serve in any part of the world, ashore or afloat.

3. Your term of Service shall begin to reckon from the date of Attestation.

4. The age given by you on enlistment will be accepted as your true age, and you will be liable to be held to serve on the engagement for which you attest notwithstanding that at some future date you may prove that your age given on enlistment is incorrect.

5. Men in receipt of a disability pension are not eligible for enlistment.

6. You will be attested by the Attesting Officer. On completion of your attestation you will be subject to all the provisions of the Air Force Act for the time being in force.

7. **You will be required by the Attestation Officer to answer the questions printed on pages 2 and 3, to take the oath shown on page 4, and you are warned that if at the time of your attestation you wilfully or knowingly make any false answer to him you**

will thereby render yourself liable under the Air Force Act to a maximum punishment of two years' imprisonment with hard labour.

8. If, after arrival at the RAF Recruits Centre, you refuse to enlist for personal reasons, you must be prepared to make your own arrangements for your return journey home. No undertaking can be given that a free warrant would be issued to you.

Interestingly, the fourth condition highlights the importance of establishing the volunteer's age, perhaps suggesting the lessons learned from the First World War, when many youngsters lied about their age in order to go off to the front with their colleagues. Also, being in bold type and underlined, the seventh condition clearly made the point about giving false information.

Once at Padgate, Les was given a medical examination, attested into the RAFVR and then sent back home on deferred service; the system had simply been overwhelmed with volunteers and he would have to wait for a little while longer. Four weeks later he received written confirmation that his enlistment into the RAFVR had been formally approved and that action would be taken to recall him from deferred service in due course. Waiting time varied from case to case and depended on when the individual volunteered and what the situation was at the time; some waited several months and, on occasions, more than a year. Fortunately, Les did not have to wait long and he received a further letter from the Air Ministry in August 1941 instructing him to proceed to the Air Crew Reception Centre (ACRC) at St John's Wood in London.

ACRCs were established across the country to receive the thousands of volunteers destined to be aircrew and it was where their training first began. The reception centre at St John's Wood was No. 3 ACRC and there were others at: Babbacombe in Torquay, Devon (No. 1 ACRC), Sale in Manchester (No. 2 ACRC), Filey (No. 4 ACRC) and

Scarborough (No. 6 ACRC), both in North Yorkshire, and another in Torquay (No. 7 ACRC). There were also two more in the Middle East: No. 1 ACRC (ME) at Jerusalem in Palestine and No. 5 ACRC (ME) at Heliopolis in Egypt.

When Les arrived at No. 3 ACRC he discovered it was located at Lord's Cricket Ground. With his fellow volunteers he was kitted out with new uniforms and given various injections. Home was a 'luxury flat' at 6 Hall Road in Maida Vale, and food was provided in Regent's Park Zoo! The days were taken up with learning how to march and attending lectures, which were sometimes given at the Swiss Cottage Odeon and included advice on how to survive in the big city of London. Marching was not limited to a parade square but involved marching in flights of thirty new recruits around the roads of St John's Wood, Maida Vale and Regent's Park. Occasionally they would be dismissed for a short break in order to buy a pint of milk and fruit pie from a passing milkman with his handcart.

The evenings were generally free, which gave the recruits the chance to enjoy London. There were many wartime clubs where a good meal could be bought for sixpence or less. For entertainment the West End shows proved popular, provided that the new recruits could afford the price; Les's pay of £1 every fortnight did not go very far in London! If a West End show was not affordable, the next best night out was dancing, and there was certainly plenty of choice. Les's favourite dance venues were the Astoria Ballroom on Charing Cross Road (which had been one of London's most popular dance venues since it first opened in 1927 and featured star acts such as Joe Loss and his band, and Jack White and his Collegians), and the Hammersmith Palais de Dance, featuring the bands of Oscar Rabin and Alf Kaplan. Les had only just celebrated his twenty-fourth birthday but he was one of the older recruits. London was, without doubt, an exciting city and, despite the risk of air raids, the days at the ACRC were remembered with great affection. It was a sad day, therefore, when the new recruits were told that their posting had come through and they were off to No. 5 Initial Training Wing (ITW) in Torquay.

A number of these wings had been set up across the country, where aircrew recruits would spend the first few weeks learning basic service training. The syllabus consisted of more drill and physical training, as well as lectures on subjects relevant to flying, such as the theory of flight, meteorology, Morse code, mathematics, navigation, aircraft recognition and airmanship. The length of training varied but was typically eight to twelve weeks. On completion of training the aircrew recruits were then sorted out for the various specializations such as pilot training, observer school, wireless school and gunnery school.

No. 5 ITW had initially been set up at Hastings but moved to Torquay in June 1940. Several aircrew passed through Torquay during the Second World War as the town's main effort was centred on providing hotels for the RAF in which to train aircrew. No. 5 ITW had its headquarters in Castle Chambers and later the Hotel Metropole, although a number of hotels were also used for training. Les was trained at the Templestowe Hotel in Tor Church Road, which was ideally located close to the town centre as well as the harbour and beach area; the hotel is still there today.

During his first leave from ITW, Les married Margaret at St Cuthbert's Church in Billingham on 8 November 1941 and so began their wonderful long life together. Then, after eight weeks of training, 1475553 Leading Aircraftman (LAC) Albert Leslie Bartlett passed out from ITW ready for posting overseas for his pilot training.

When the Second World War broke out there was a defficit of more than 1,000 pilots under training. This led to a huge demand for pilot training facilities, which meant that more airfields were needed as well as more aircraft and equipment. The combination of insufficient resources, uncertain weather and the threat of constant interference by the *Luftwaffe* meant that an alternative arrangement was required. Provisional plans had already been put in place during the mid-to late 1930s, initially with Canada, for pilots to undergo training overseas. This led to the Empire Air Training Scheme, later to be called the British Commonwealth Air Training Plan, which was a four-nation agreement between the UK, Canada, Australia and New Zealand. The UK had also been conducting talks with South Africa, Southern Rhodesia and the United States of America to allow aircrew training to be conducted in those countries as well. The first overseas flying training schools were in operation by early 1940 and all the schools planned by the scheme were in operation by the end of 1941. In the case of South Africa, an agreement was signed on 1 June 1940 to run for the duration of the war, with the RAF aircrew going out to South Africa after ITW where they would learn to fly alongside South African Air Force (SAAF) cadets.

When 1941 came to a close, Les did not know exactly where he was to go overseas, or for how long. The Christmas and New Year period was more special than ever for the newly-weds. Throughout Les's time at the ACRC and the ITW, Margaret had remained in the north-east where she had been working as a secretary to the Transport Manager at the United Bus Depot in Middlesbrough. Les was then sent to a transit camp in Blackpool for ten days. Margaret managed to get a week's leave to be near him and Les put her up in a boarding house in Albert Road, not far from his billet. As it happened, apart from a roll call every morning, he was free for the rest of the day and he was able to spend most of his time with Margaret. Whilst Blackpool in a cold February might not have appealed to everyone, the time was precious.

Then the call came. It was about midnight when Les was told to pack up his belongings and be ready to move in an hour's time. Before he knew it he had said his goodbyes and was on a train heading north to Scotland. Margaret was left to find her own way back to Middlesbrough! Although Les did not know it at the time, it would be fifteen months before he and Margaret would see each other again.

By the end of February 1942 the world was well and truly at war. Japan's entry had brought in the United States and the war had spread to the Far East with the fall of Malaya and Singapore. Germany's invasion of the Soviet Union during the previous spring meant that the Eastern Front was rapidly becoming the biggest theatre of the war. In North Africa Rommel had counter-attacked as the British Army fell back towards Tobruk as the pendulum in the Western Desert campaign swung once more. In the Mediterranean the tiny fortress island of Malta was only just hanging on for survival. Closer to home the German occupation of Western and Central Europe remained unchallenged. At sea there were heavy losses for the Royal Navy during the Mediterranean and Arctic convoys but success against the German U-boats in the Battle of the Atlantic meant that vital convoys were arriving in Britain.

February 1942 also marked a period of change and the turning point of the war for Bomber Command. After frequent changes of commander, it acquired at its head the man who was to inspire and lead it for the rest of the war, Air Marshal Arthur 'Bomber' Harris. For some time, Harris had been concerned about the way the bombing offensive was being conducted. He was convinced of the value, and the necessity, of bombing but its decisive nature should not be misused or bled away to other areas. The entry into the war of the United States brought American heavy bombers and aircrew to Britain, which allowed Bomber Command to intensify its night bombing campaign against Germany. The appointment of Arthur Harris at the head of Bomber Command undoubtedly gave a tremendous boost to its morale at a time when its fortunes and spirits were at a low ebb.

This period also proved significant for Bomber Command for another reason. On the night of 3/4 March 1942, four of its newest heavy bombers, Avro Lancasters, from No. 44 Sqn based at Waddington, took part in mine-laying operations in the Heligoland approaches; all four returned safely. The speed at which the Lancaster had entered operational service was quite remarkable considering that its predecessor, the twin-engine Avro Manchester, had made its first operational flight just twelve months before. The decision was made to re-equip all of the heavy bomber squadrons in No. 5 Group with the new Lancaster and by the end of March 1942 the number of Manchester squadrons was reduced to just three. One of the early squadrons to take delivery of the Lancaster during March was No. 50 Sqn based at Skellingthorpe near Lincoln, which then commenced operations with the aircraft on the night of 8/9 April.

After his long train journey to Scotland, Les stood on the quayside at Greenock on the Firth of Clyde early the next morning. Staring silently at the SS *Ormonde* alongside, reliving in his mind the events of the past ten days, the aches and pains of the overnight train journey slowly eased. It was overcast and there was a strong wind blowing. Much had happened during the past ten months, from walking into the recruiting office in Middlesbrough to standing on the quay-side about to depart overseas. After all the wondering and speculation about where he might be going, Les had learned that it was to be South Africa. He did not dwell for too long on what the coming months and years might bring; he was, after all, a willing volunteer!

CHAPTER TWO

South Africa

Built by the Orient Lines in 1917, the SS *Ormonde* had served as a troopship between the wars, its regular route being from the UK, through Suez, to Australia. She would later return to commercial service after the war before she was finally scrapped in Scotland in 1952, but for the next six weeks she was to be home for Les. Embarkation began almost immediately, and during the night the ship moved from the quayside to an anchorage awaiting orders to sail and form a convoy. Accommodation was on mess decks with lines of mess tables reaching from the hull towards the centre of the ship. Each table accommodated twelve airmen to eat. Above the tables were hammocks held to the ceiling by large hooks; this was not the Ritz!

The *Ormonde* sailed under cover of darkness and formed a convoy. When it reached the Irish Sea it was blowing a gale and the ship was rolling and pitching; faces were white or green. Having eaten his first dinner on board, Les felt most uncomfortable, and the smell on the mess deck was quite nauseating. He went up on deck to get some fresh air but was immediately sick. It was evident that down below was not the place to be and he was joined by many others. Les looked around to find some shelter from the rain. There was a tarpaulin, the cover of a Bofors gun, lying on the deck and he crawled under it. There he stayed, cared for by a friend who brought him bread and the odd amount of food.

On the second day Les was slowly finding his sea legs and

was able to venture below, although not for long. At the end of each mess table a 40 gallon oil drum had been placed, 'airmen, for the use of', but they had broken loose during the gale and were now rolling about the deck; the stench was indescribable, so he beat a hasty retreat.

By the fourth day it was all change. The sky was blue, the sea was green and the wind had changed to a relatively mild breeze. There was much cleaning up to do but gradually conditions got back to normal. Les was starting to find the experience of being at sea quite interesting. They were in the Atlantic, surrounded by about thirty other ships, with an escort of destroyers, cruisers and an aircraft carrier. However, little did they realize the dangers to which they were now exposed. They were in U-boat territory, and the submarines were known to be hunting in packs; orders were given to keep lifejackets available at all times.

For a few days the new seafarers tried to get to grips with their hammocks, but as they reached warmer climes they started sleeping out on deck with their blankets and just went below for meals. After two weeks at sea Les asked one of the galley crew why curry was served so frequently; the answer was along the lines of 'Well, mate, you wouldn't like it if you could see the maggots would you?'

The trip to Durban took six weeks with a few days spent at anchor in Freetown to take on supplies of water and fresh food, and it was April 1942 when Les arrived in South Africa to attend No. 2 Air School at Randfontein in the Transvaal. It was in the western suburbs of Johannesburg but the train journey from Durban was hardly direct; in fact, it took about three days to complete. The train was one of the standard troop trains, which headed south along the eastern coastline through the eastern Cape Province before heading inland and then north towards Johannesburg, stopping at various stations along the way to take on food for the troops and water for the engine. Occasionally it would have a longer stop to allow faster trains to overtake. One of these stops was at a station between East London and King William's Town in the

Eastern Cape Province. To everyone's surprise the station was at a small settlement called Berlin. The temptation to have a photograph taken on the platform was too great. The memory of this chance opportunity to acquaint himself with another Berlin has remained with Les and the photograph taken by his friend at the time has always had a special place in his photograph album.

Randfontein was established on a farm owned by Louis le Grange when gold was first found in the area in 1889. The town was initially part of the Krugersdorp municipality, but became an independent town in 1929. No. 2 Air School was one of a number of air training schools in South Africa, which together trained some 25,000 aircrew during the Second World War. It was where pilots completed the first stage of their pilot training, known as elementary flying training, which generally consisted of about fifty flying hours on the De Havilland Tiger Moth and lasted about three months. The flying instructors were from the SAAF, although there were a few RAF officers in various posts, including the Chief Flying Instructor.

The DH82 Tiger Moth was an excellent training aircraft which had first been delivered to the RAF in 1932. By the outbreak of the Second World War more than 1,000 were in service with the RAF at home and many more were located overseas. It was to be the last biplane *ab-initio* trainer to be used by the RAF but, although the open cockpit proved cold and draughty in climates other than South Africa, the aircraft proved to be extremely robust and relatively easy to fly. The variant at Randfontein was the DH82A Tiger Moth II, which was powered by a Gipsy Major I engine and gave it a maximum speed of around 100 mph and a ceiling of just over 13,000ft.

Les was put on 'A' Flight and his first training flight was in the early morning of 26 May 1942. His instructor was Lieutenant Goldschmidt of the SAAF and his first training sortie was a simple air experience flight and cockpit familiarization, with the aim of getting the young pupil used to his new 'office' in the airborne environment. The sortie lasted just forty minutes but it was an unforgettable experience; it was, after all, the first time Les had been airborne in his life and the view of Johannesburg from the air was truly memorable. The next three training sorties that week involved how to taxi the aircraft, the effects of controls, engine handling, flying straight and level, climbing, gliding, stalling and turning both with and without engine power. By the end of his first week Les had flown six times and he had learned how to take off; the learning curve for any new pilot was steep to say the least.

The next two weeks were much the same and on 11 June he was ready to go solo. Although only ten minutes long every pilot remembers his first solo and later in his life, when listing his most memorable moments during his flying career, Les placed going solo on the Tiger Moth first – a truly unforgettable experience. The next week was spent consolidating what he had learned, much of which was solo, and during the next three months he was introduced to more advanced handling, such as spinning, steep turns, side-slipping, precautionary and forced landings, instrument flying, aerobatics and night flying. Sorties were typically only twenty to thirty minutes long with generally two or three trips a day. Les was extremely keen but it was undoubtedly hard work.

When off-duty and at the weekends time was free, and Les thoroughly enjoyed his experience of being in South Africa; the weather was good, the food was excellent and there was plenty of cheap wine and brandy. There were several service clubs in Johannesburg which were for the benefit of RAF personnel wishing to see what life was like in South Africa. Les was, as always, keen to make the most of the experience and one Friday afternoon he visited one of the clubs and expressed a wish to visit a typical farm on the veld. The receptionist took his name and asked him to take a seat while she made a few phone calls. You can imagine his surprise when she came back and said that if he returned at 4 p.m. Mrs Bartlett will collect him and take him to their farm near Vereeniging, about 30 miles south of Johannesburg. This coincidence of surname was both curious and exciting, and led to a memorable relationship during his stay in South Africa. As requested, Les returned and was introduced to Kay Bartlett. When he expressed his concern at going so far away from Johannesburg Kay told him that her husband, Phil, would take him back at whatever time necessary; she explained that her husband had a furniture factory just outside Johannesburg and would be able to drop Les off so that he could be back on duty at Randfontein on Monday morning.

The farmhouse at Koedoesfontein Farm was beautiful and built entirely with timber from the factory, all African hardwoods. In the grounds next to the swimming pool there was a guesthouse which could accommodate six people, and later Les would often take his friends there. The farm had a staff of ten farmhands. Kay had a maid and a cook and Phil a manservant. Les was often able to drive one of their cars, either a Cadillac or a Buick, and the war seemed a world away. All of his off-duty time was spent on the farm and he quickly became accepted as 'one of the family'. When he was flying solo he often flew his Tiger Moth over to the farm and practised his aerobatics, with the occasional low flypast thrown in for good measure!

By the end of September 1942 Les had completed his elementary flying training with eighty-six training flights totalling sixty-one hours in his log book; he flew his final test on the morning of 28 September with the Chief Flying Instructor, Squadron Leader Winton, who commented that his flying was erratic and he spent too much time flying on instruments and not enough time looking around. The one thing a pilot would need to have the capacity to do in any operational theatre was to keep a good lookout!

Unfortunately for Les, he had also developed a condition brought on by the state of the airfield, which required medical attention. The airfield at Randfontein was rough, sandy scrub and very uneven. When not detailed for flying, the under training (U/T) pilots were ordered to assist those who were flying by taking taxiing duty, one on each wing tip, to avoid damage to the Tiger Moth because of the state of the airfield. When the aircraft was in position the pilot turned into wind, opened the throttle and took off. This caused a shower of dust, sand and dirt, which completely enveloped those assisting. As a result Les developed *seborrhoea dermatitis* in his scalp. Treatment by the station Medical Officer proved unsuccessful so instead of progressing to the Senior Flying Training School at Standerton with the rest of his course he found himself heading for Johannesburg General Hospital instead.

Four weeks later he was discharged but in the meantime had lost all his hair. His scalp came away in patches, which, when held up to the light, showed lots of tiny holes where hair had been. Les was resigned to being bald for the rest of his life and was given two weeks' sick leave, which he enjoyed in the Royal Hotel in Durban. By the time he returned to Randfontein once more he had been away for a total of six weeks. He had already noticed that things were very quiet on the station when the Commanding Officer sent for him. It is fair to say that Les was not a natural pilot but he had completed elementary flying training, although his future was now in the balance.

The problem he faced was that there was no way he could catch up with the rest of his course at Standerton but there were no more U/T pilots arriving at Randfontein in the foreseeable future for him to join up with. Simply put, his days as a pilot were over, which meant that he and his Commanding Officer were now faced with deciding what should happen next. Eventually, the decision was made that he would go to Port Elizabeth for the air bombers' course. Having said his goodbyes to the Bartletts, he made his way to Port Elizabeth, where he joined No. 6 Air Bombers' Course in November 1942.

Port Elizabeth is in the eastern Cape region. The landscape is diverse, from arid and desolate to lush green, and the sandy beaches along Algoa Bay and the Indian Ocean has always made it a popular location. The air school was at Port

Elizabeth airport, which had been built on the western side of the city during the early 1930s to operate a postal service between Port Elizabeth and Cape Town. When it officially opened in 1936 it had a single runway, one hangar and a concrete apron. During the opening period of the war the facilities had to be extended on the southern side of the airfield to accommodate No. 42 Air School for the RAF and on the eastern side of the airfield to accommodate No. 6 Sqn SAAF; commercial operations were conducted from the northern side of the airfield.

No. 6 Air Bomber's Course had twenty members and training would last about three months. As at Randfontein, the instructors at Port Elizabeth were from the SAAF. Les flew his first training sortie at Port Elizabeth on 28 November, which lasted one hour and twenty five minutes. His pilot was Lieutenant Jackson and it was another of those air experience flights. On this occasion, of course, he already had sixty-one hours of flying experience behind him and the aircraft he was in was an Airspeed Oxford. The twin-engined trainer was powered by Cheetah engines, which gave it a speed of around 180mph and an operating ceiling up to 19,000ft. The Oxford had first entered service in 1937. It had a crew of three and the training sorties lasted typically one and a half to two and a half hours.

Although called an air bombers' course, the students were taught navigation, bombing and air gunnery. Some of the training sorties were dedicated to learning navigation techniques, some bombing techniques, some navigation and bombing combined, and some air gunnery. The two different types of aircraft used at the school for the air bombers were the Airspeed Oxford and the Avro Anson; the Anson was similar in size and performance to the Oxford and typically carried a crew of three or four for training.

Les's next sortie was on 5 December, when he was taught the art of understanding wind speed and direction, a challenge for generations of navigators; it was flown in the Oxford. His introduction to the Anson came the following day, the sortie was more than two hours long and was the first of his combined navigation/bombing instructional outings. The course members enjoyed a few days off over the Christmas period but there was to be no let-up over the New Year, with training flights on both New Year's Eve and New Year's Day. They were then introduced to night techniques during January, which would for most become the 'bread and butter' for their forthcoming tour of operations. The end of the month and early February saw an introduction to air gunnery, which was carried out on the Oxford as it was fitted with an Armstrong Whitworth AW23 gun turret behind the cockpit.

The AW23 was an early design gun turret and was manually operated, but it nonetheless proved popular with the trainees. When fitted to the Oxford or Anson the turret had a full 360 degree rotation, with an elevation of 87 degrees and a depression of 85. This caused the occasional accidental damage to the aircraft when a bullet hole from the Lewis or Vickers gun was found through the tail or wings!

By the end of the course in February 1943, Les had flown nearly fifty-five hours on the Oxford and the Anson, which was broken down approximately as follows: fifteen hours' navigation flying, thirty hours' bombing and ten hours' gunnery, with about one-third of the flying carried out at night. As with all courses, its members had become very close during their time together but tragically half of them would not live to see the end of the war.

Having added sergeant's stripes and an air bomber's brevet to his uniform, Les left Port Elizabeth and travelled to Cape Town to await transport back to the UK. Once at Cape Town he found himself quickly settling in to a new daily routine, which was to report to the Transport Officer each morning at 10 a.m. to see if he was on the next troopship sailing for the UK, and then the rest of the day was free. Whilst in Cape Town most of his time was spent on the glorious beaches of Simonstown and Muisenburg enjoying picnics of South African food and wine; again, the war seemed a world away.

However, it all came to an end on the night of 13 March 1943, when Les boarded the United States troopship *Mariposa* and was finally on his way back to the UK.

Built by the Bethlehem Shipbuilding Corporation in Quincy, USA, the *Mariposa* was used as a luxurious ocean cruise liner between San Francisco, Honolulu and Sydney before the war. More than 18,000 tons and 630ft in length, it had two funnels, two masts, was twin-screw and was capable of twenty-two knots. As a cruise liner the ship could accommodate 745 first class and 229 cabin class passengers. Since 1941 it had been used as a US Navy transport ship and memories of the return journey from South Africa were far better than the outward journey a year earlier; not only was it a considerably faster voyage but the facilities on board were superb and the food served by the American crew was never to be forgotten. They sailed unescorted back to Clyde, arriving in just fourteen days. During meal times everyone was issued with a stainless steel tray which had six separate compartments. First was the starter, which could be either a fried breakfast or a fish or cheese dish, depending on what time it was in the morning. Next was the main course, which was usually meat or poultry with a selection of vegetables, often fresh. Last there was a selection of sweets and a variety of fresh fruit, and, of course, plenty of ice cream. There were two meals a day, morning and evening, and at the end of each it was possible to take away as much food as possible.

After disembarking Les boarded the troop train which was waiting at the quayside and he settled down to being back home. When passing through Glasgow the train came to a standstill on a bridge overlooking one of the main thorough-fares. Keen to attract the attention of the locals, someone threw down an orange and there was a mad scramble to get it. The traffic came to a standstill and there were plenty of cheers from the locals as more oranges were thrown from the train. It was a timely reminder for those returning from South Africa that there was a war on and, although plentiful in South Africa and on the troopship home, fresh fruit such as an orange was still very much a luxury back home.

As darkness fell the train was blacked out and so no one had any idea where it was heading. About 3 a.m. it came to a halt in a station and the passengers opened the windows to see if there were any clues as to where they were. The station was in complete darkness and not a soul was in sight when on to the platform walked a figure. Les shouted to ask where they were and he could not believe his ears when he heard the reply, 'Darlington, mate', he was just 11 miles from where Margaret was living. Les called him over and asked him if he would be good enough to ring his wife and tell her that he was safely back from South Africa. He quickly scribbled her phone number on a piece of paper, stuffed a ten shilling note into his hand and told him to have a drink with the change. The train moved on and eventually arrived at their final destination, Harrogate. At the first opportunity Les rang Margaret and she told him that the complete stranger had stuck to his word and had called her at 3.30 a.m. with the good news.

For the next month home was at the Grand Hotel in Harrogate. It gave Les and Margaret some long overdue time together. Les soon found out that his next posting was to Jurby on the Isle of Man, which Margaret pointed out was overseas once again!

CHAPTER THREE

So Much to Learn

The RAF airfield at Jurby was situated on the north-west coast of the Isle of Man and initially opened in September 1939 as No. 5 Bombing and Gunnery School. In July 1941 it was renamed No. 5 Air Observer School (AOS), equipped with Ansons, Henleys and Hampdens, and by the time Les arrived on 9 May 1943 the unit also had Blenheims. Whilst at No. 5 AOS, Les was taught advanced navigation and bombing techniques, and some more air gunnery on the Avro Anson and Bristol Blenheim. His first sortie was in an Anson on 14 May, during which he was taught more techniques for calculating wind speed and direction; the trip lasted two hours. It was to be a long day as he flew two more Anson sorties, learning more bombing techniques.

The course was, indeed, intense. He flew two more training bombing sorties on the 16th and two more on the 17th. The following day he flew a map-reading sortie to Hooton Park in Liverpool with his pilot, Warrant Officer Harrington. They landed for a turn-round before returning to Jurby later in the day. There was to be no rest, as on the following day, 19 May, he flew his first two gunnery training sorties in the Blenheim, and the following night he flew a night map-reading training sortie in the Anson. The course ended on 31 May and his last three trips were all night-training sorties in the Anson, flown on consecutive nights between 25 and 27 May, during which he had to complete a night map-reading exercise into the simulated bombing of a target. During the course he had flown a further thirty-six hours consisting of fifteen sorties in the Anson, including four at night, and five day sorties in the Blenheim, during which he had fired a total of 400 rounds.

The next stop on the seemingly never ending training road was No. 14 Operational Training Unit (OTU) at Cottesmore, his first posting to a Bomber Command station. When Bomber Command was established in 1936 it took over an organization and basic structure that had essentially been in existence since the mid-1920s but was then in the process of changing from a small-scale force of light and medium day bombers to a night-capable and eventually heavier bombing force. To appreciate the problems facing the operational training organization, it is important to understand that there was more to expanding the bomber force than merely building more bombers. The main problem was how to increase the trained manpower, not only the aircrew but the ground crew as well. To illustrate the point, the standard day bomber of the mid-1930s was the two-seat Hawker Hind. A typical bomber squadron comprised up to twenty pilots plus the wireless operator/air gunners. Working on the assumption that there were twenty squadrons, with each squadron turning over half of its pilots each year, the training organization needed to provide 200 pilots a year.

During the build-up to the Second World War, doubling the number of squadrons doubled the task. There was also the question of where the additional instructors would come from in order to meet the training task; taking them from the squadrons merely increased the task further, and so there became a circle of ever-diminishing returns. Furthermore, the length of time taken to train a bomber pilot was on average nearly eighteen months; therefore a system would have to be in place at least eighteen months before the start of any hostilities.

With the introduction of the new heavier bombers, the decision was made that two pilots were required for each aircraft and so the task doubled again and the drain of experienced pilots from the front-line squadrons increased.

Then there was the fact that the new bombers had a crew of six or seven, each with his own specialization. It is therefore easy to see just how big the training task was for Bomber Command alone, without even considering the other commands. It was eventually realized that the only solution was to reduce the front-line strength by allocating certain squadrons, and experienced aircrew, as training units. These squadrons became the operational training units; for example, No. 14 OTU at Cottesmore was formed from No. 185 Sqn, which at the time was a Hampden squadron operating from the station. The OTUs tended to be equipped with either older aircraft or aircraft no longer suitable for operational service, which meant that the training units were last in line when it came to receiving spares and modifications. These problems faced by Bomber Command were immense and the provision of trained aircrew to its squadrons is one of its rarely recognized achievements.

By the time that Les arrived on No. 14 OTU at Cottesmore, it was June 1943 and it was two years since he had first attested into the RAFVR. The excitement undoubtedly increased as he could now see a flickering light at the end of what had seemed a very long tunnel. Located about 10 miles north-west of Stamford, just to the north of Rutland Water, Cottesmore had opened as an airfield of No. 2 Group Bomber Command a year before the outbreak of the Second World War. The airfield had initially been home to Vickers Wellesleys of No. 35 Sqn and Fairey Battles of No. 207 Sqn but by September 1939 it had been transferred to No. 5 Group Bomber Command and was home to two squadrons of Handley Page Hampdens; No. 106 Sqn and No. 185 Sqn.

Soon after the war broke out it was decided that Cottesmore would no longer be a front-line Bomber Command station and so, once again, command and control of the airfield was transferred, this time to No. 6 (Training) Group with the role of training crews for Bomber Command. The rapid increase in the number of bomber crews required led to many new units being formed. No. 14 OTU was formed in April 1940, using the Hampdens of No. 185 Sqn as well as receiving Avro Ansons and Handley Page Herefords – more than seventy aircraft in all.

The training task at Cottesmore increased throughout the next two years. The unit also provided aircraft and crews for operations when all available assets were required. One example was the first Thousand Bomber raid against Cologne on the night of 30/1 May 1942, when twenty-nine Hampdens and crews from No. 14 OTU at Cottesmore took part in the raid; three aircraft failed to return. One young Bomber Command pilot taking part in the raid that night was Flying Officer Leslie Manser of No. 50 Sqn based at RAF Skelling-thorpe. Whilst approaching Cologne his Avro Manchester had been caught in searchlights and seriously damaged by flak. Manser had managed to complete his bombing run before turning for home, although his aircraft continued to lose height. There was no chance of reaching safety and so Manser ordered his crew to bale out. He held the aircraft steady for just long enough to enable the crew to bale out but in doing so had no chance to save his own life. The Man-chester crashed near the Belgian village of Bree with the gallant pilot still on board. Although he had just celebrated his twentieth birthday he had demonstrated courage and maturity beyond his years. For his gallant action, Leslie Manser was posthumously awarded the Victoria Cross. He was buried in the Heverlee War Cemetery in Belgium. The significance of both Leslie Manser and No. 50 Sqn will become clear later.

Although forty-one aircraft were lost on the Cologne raid, this represented less than 4 per cent of the bombers that took part and the raid was considered a success. Interestingly, the OTU losses were less than those of the main force squadrons and the student crews that had taken part in the raid suffered fewer losses than the instructor crews. The second Thousand Bomber raid took place just two nights later against Essen and the third and final one on the night of 25/26 June against Bremen. Again, more than twenty Hampdens from Cottesmore took part in each raid, with the loss of just one aircraft against Bremen. The second and third raids were less successful, the OTUs in particular suffered heavy losses against Bremen, but these Thousand Bomber raids marked another great achievement for Arthur Harris and Bomber Command. However, these massive efforts could not be sustained, and Bomber Command reverted to using smaller numbers of bombers on the raids and the OTUs returned to concentrating on their training task, although they did take part in main force raids when required.

By June 1943, No. 14 OTU was equipped with a mix of Wellingtons, Ansons and Oxfords but Cottesmore's task as a wartime training establishment was beginning to draw to a close. During the previous year alone the station had trained more than 1,000 bomber aircrew but preparations were now being made for the construction of new concrete runways, which were required for the new and heavier aircraft about to enter service. This meant that Les's course would only stay at Cottesmore for three weeks before No. 14 OTU was moved to a new location.

For the students the OTU was a different world from the previous training schools. Up until that point the student had generally been trained in the individual skills that he would require in his forthcoming tour of operations but it was the task of the OTU to develop those skills and to mould the students into capable bomber crews. One of its most important purposes was to find the right mix of individuals who would 'gel' together to work professionally and effectively as an operational bomber crew. In the first instance this was left to the individuals, the brief being that they should form themselves into crews. Some naturally gravitated towards each other, perhaps having met before at various stages of their training, and others joined by recommendation; those remaining would be allocated by the instructors.

The OTU syllabus was intended to provide the crew with basic handling and operational skills. Most of the instructors were on rest tours between operations and therefore able to pass on the benefits of their experience. The course length varied but was typically up to eighty hours for the pilots with the other crew specializations getting about forty hours. By 1943 it had been decided that only one pilot would be in each heavy bomber crew and the new specialization of bomb aimer had been introduced, thus reducing the workload of the navigator. With two air gunners and a wireless operator, the basic heavy bomber crew had stood at six but another new specialization, the flight engineer, had been introduced during the previous summer, which brought the total to seven.

Les flew his first training sortie with No. 14 OTU in an Avro Anson on the night of 17 June 1943. The sortie was a map reading exercise, which lasted for two hours and forty-five minutes. As he was familiar with both the Anson and flying at night, this proved to be a straightforward exercise. It was at this stage of his training that Les met up with the colleagues that formed the nucleus of the crew that would eventually go on to the Lancaster.

Because the OTU training was to be carried out on the Vickers Wellington, the crew was made up of five members: Pilot Officer Mike Beetham (pilot), Pilot Officer Frank Swinyard (navigator), Sergeant Reg Payne (wireless operator), Sergeant Fred Ball (rear gunner) and Les (bomb aimer).

When he arrived at Cottesmore, Mike Beetham had only just celebrated his twentieth birthday. Born on 17 May 1923 and educated at St Marylebone Grammar School, his father had served as an infantry officer during the First World War but had been recalled following the outbreak of the Second World War to run a training battalion near Portsmouth. Whilst at home during his summer holiday in 1940, Mike Beetham had watched the Battle of Britain unfold in the skies over southern England and he immediately decided that he wanted to join the RAF as a pilot rather than follow his father into the army. As soon as he was eighteen years old, he volunteered for pilot training and joined the RAF in 1941. Following his initial training at Scarborough and flying grading at Perth in Scotland, he went to the USA to complete his pilot training. Although he had the opportunity to remain in the USA as an instructor, he wanted to become operational and so he returned to the UK, where he trained on Airspeed Oxfords at No. 18 Advanced Flying Unit (AFU) before being posted to No. 14 OTU at Cottesmore.

The second commissioned officer and the oldest member of the crew was the navigator, Frank Swinyard. Born on 1 April 1916 at the Manor House, Finsbury Park, in London, Frank Swinyard had moved with his family to Luton, where he attended Luton Modern School. He was a keen sportsman and had worked as assistant to the Company Secretary at High Duty Alloys in Slough before volunteering for the RAF.

The second youngest member of the crew by just a few weeks was the wireless operator, Reg Payne. Born on 11 March 1923, Reg went to school in Kettering. As a young boy he was keen on outdoor activities, mainly camping during the summer months and learning to swim in the local river, playing football and building model aircraft. He left school at the age of fourteen and worked as a junior records clerk for the British Legion. When war broke out he was still only sixteen years old and too young for active service. He joined the local Defence Volunteers as soon as he was seventeen years old and then volunteered for the RAF when he was seventeen and a half. Having been classed as suitable for wireless operator/air gunner training he was trained at RAF Blackpool Squire and RAF Yatesbury during late 1941 and early 1942. After spendng some time on ground duties he was then sent to RAF Hadeley in January 1943 for airborne wireless training in Proctors and Dominies. He then carried out his air gunnery course at Storny Down in Wales, at the end of which he was promoted to the rank of sergeant. After a short advanced course at Wigtown, in Scotland, he was posted to Cottesmore, where he joined up with the others on the OTU.

The fifth member of the new crew was Fred Ball, who was twenty-two years old and came from a large Roman Catholic family in Birmingham. He was the youngest son of a family of twelve and had been employed in the jewellery business in Birmingham before the war. His main interests were simple: cigarettes and a game of cards. And so, the five young men came together and immediately started to bond as a group. What the next year would bring was uncertain but each one of them felt ready for the challenge.

The following week Les flew his first sortie in the Wellington, a daytime practice air gunnery sortie, which lasted just an hour. The Wellington had first flown in 1936 and its excellent payload and performance made it, without doubt, the most important bomber of the early war years. Fourteen Wellingtons had taken part in the first bombing mission on 4 September 1939 and from that moment on it had shouldered the Bomber Command offensive until the introduction of the four-engined heavies. By 1943 its contribution to the main force operations had reduced and the last operation was flown on the night of 8/9 October 1943.

Les's next training sortie was flown on 27 June. This was his second Wellington sortie and his first with Mike Beetham, who had Flying Officer Hamer checking him out, and the rest of his new crew. The check ride lasted just an hour, after which the new 'sprog' crew flew solo for the first time. Having flown twice that day, and as a crew for the first time, there was much to celebrate and from that point on all their training sorties on the OTU would be flown on the Wellington and all as a junior crew.

With Cottesmore's wartime training task over, No. 14 OTU moved the short distance up the road to RAF Saltby. It was the end of June and Les was just five sorties into the OTU course. RAF Saltby was about 10 miles south-west of Grantham, to the west of the main A1 road between London and the north, and south of the Grantham – Melton Mowbray road. This move was only temporary as the OTU was destined for another Leicestershire airfield at Market Harborough. However, whilst at Saltby during July the crew flew a further thirteen training sorties: eight by day and five at night. The daytime training varied from local familiarization sorties to cross-country navigation exercises, which resulted in a simulated bombing run against a target; these training sorties, in particular, brought all the crew's skills together. The night training sorties were a mix of circuits and landings at the airfield, as well as some high-level simulated bombing sorties.

In early August the OTU moved to RAF Market Harborough, a newly constructed airfield located about 1 mile to the north-west of the town, near the village of Foxton. The airfield had only opened three months before and had a satellite airfield at Husbands Bosworth 5 miles to the south-west.

No. 14 OTU was the first unit to operate from Market Harborough. Les and his crew flew their first local familiarization sortie from the airfield on 15 August; it lasted just over an hour. Two days later they were airborne again, this time on a cross-country exercise, which resulted in a simulated bombing attack against a target; the sortie lasted for four hours and fifty minutes, his longest training sortie to date. The crew then had a few days off before the next training sortie, which was similar to the previous but carried out at night.

Unsurprisingly, the night sorties became the 'bread and butter' of the course and generally lasted in excess of three hours. Not only did they last longer as the course progressed but the rate increased. This was not only to put pressure on the crew but also to make up for lost time due to the number of moves between airfields. The last eight days of the course were as follows (flight times in hours and minutes are in brackets): 23 August – night cross-country (3:20), 24 August – day fighter affiliation (0:55), 25 August – night cross-country (3:05), 27 August – day night-flying test (0:40) followed by night cross-country (1:25), 30 August – day night-flying test (0:55) followed by one night cross-country (3:30) and a second night cross-country (2:30), 31 August – night cross-country, final training sortie (5:30).

To summarize the two weeks at Market Harborough, the crew carried out eight and a half hours of day flying and nearly twenty hours of night flying. At the end of the course Les had flown just over sixty hours; the split between day and night flying was exactly equal. He had been trained in navigation, bombing and air gunnery and on his Form 414(A) Summary of Flying and Assessments for the course in his log book, the officer commanding No. 14 OTU assessed Les as 'average' for all three disciplines; it was 1 September 1943.

Les celebrated his twenty-sixth birthday just three days before starting the next, and final, phase of training. There had been a double celebration as the crew's pilot, Mike Beetham, had just been promoted to the rank of flying officer. If it had not already dawned on the crew that they were all just a matter of a few weeks away from the start of their operational tour, then it certainly did now.

The introduction of the new four-engine heavies had brought many problems as they were quite different from the Whitleys and Wellingtons being flown at the OTUs. Initially, an additional four aircraft per Bomber Command squadron were provided as a mini-conversion flight but this solution was far from ideal, as the squadrons were not established as training units and the level of instruction was variable. The next stage was to combine these extra aircraft into conversion flights for each bomber group, which, again, was not ideal. Finally, the Heavy Conversion Units (HCUs) were born, the idea being that the crews could then convert to the type ready for their operational tour. The early exception to this was the Lancaster, where initially all available aircraft were required by the squadrons and so the crews went to a Lancaster finishing school for a short introduction to the aircraft.

No. 1654 HCU was based at RAF Wigsley 5 miles to the west of Lincoln but just within the boundaries of Nottinghamshire. The airfield had opened early in 1942 as a satellite airfield for nearby Swinderby, which was one of No. 5 Group's main operational bases. No. 1654 HCU was the first Lancaster heavy conversion unit, having been formed in May 1942. The unit moved to Wigsley the following month and it was responsible for the training of aircrew after the OTU, by converting them on to four-engined types and finally preparing them for their operational tour with one of the squadrons in No. 5 Group.

It was at Wigsley that the Beetham crew of five became a crew of seven, when Sergeants Don Moore (flight engineer) and Jock Higgins (rear gunner) joined up with Les and his colleagues to make the full Lancaster crew.

The two additional crew members were quite different. Don Moore was from London and in his late twenties. A mature family man he was married with a young child and had gained much knowledge of aircraft engines, having worked as an engine fitter in the RAF before he volunteered for flight engineer training. Ian Higgins was quite the opposite. Coming from Glasgow he was unsurprisingly known as 'Jock' and was very much the single man who had quickly developed a reputation with the ladies. And so, the Beetham crew was complete; it was as diverse a crew as you could expect to see and not at all untypical of Bomber Command crews at the time.

During the period in 1943 that Les and the crew went through training, No. 1654 HCU was equipped with Lancasters and Halifaxes. Powered by four Rolls-Royce Merlin engines the Handley Page Halifax had been the second of the new heavies to enter service, making its operational debut in March 1941, just one month behind the Short Stirling. Although the Halifax had suffered higher than average losses on operations it had proved to be a sturdy and reliable aircraft and was generally well liked by its crews.

The crew's first training sortie on the HCU was flown in a Halifax on 20 September and involved two and a half hours of 'circuits and bumps'. Whilst this was no easy ride for Mike Beetham, as the Halifax required careful handling during any hard manoeuvres, the sortie like any other 'circuits and bumps' sortie became somewhat tedious for the rest of the crew. There was, however, the added attraction of flying in yet another new type; for Les, this was to be his one and only trip in a Halifax.

The next sortie, on 24 September, was to be an unforgettable one for the crew as it was their first flight in a Lancaster.
This was the mainstay of Bomber Command's effort during
the latter half of the Second World War. It was born out of its
twin-engined predecessor, the Avro Manchester, and had
first flown in January 1941. The Lancaster was powered by
four Rolls-Royce Merlin XX engines. It was nearly 70ft in
length, had a wing span of over 100ft and, when fully loaded,
weighed 65,000lb at take-off. This gave it an operational
ceiling of more than 24,000ft and an operational range of
more than 1,600 miles. In all, 7,377 Lancasters were built and
it went on to serve with more than eighty different squadrons
throughout its operational career.

The actual aircraft flown by the Beetham crew for their first
flight was R5910, which was a Lancaster Mk I built by
Metropolitan-Vickers. It was one of nearly 1,000 Mk Is built at
Trafford Park and Mosley Road, and R5910 was one of the
first batch of fifty-seven aircraft delivered into service during
early 1942. The sortie was a dual familiarization for Mike
Beetham and the crew, which again lasted two and a half
hours. The next sortie was on 28 September, again another
dual for Mike Beetham, which involved countless circuits and
lasted just over an hour.

The crew were now checked out as competent to go solo
and, on 2 October, the day came. Like any first solo for a pilot
on a new aircraft type, the time taken to crew in, start up and
get airborne by far exceeds the amount of time spent in the
air. Mike Beetham carried out the engine start checks: check
the brake pressure, check the idle cut-off, switch the
ground/flight switch to 'ground', pull the boost cut-out lever
up, switch on the undercarriage warning lights and flap indicators, set the supercharger, open the throttles to
three-quarters, lock the undercarriage, close the bomb doors,
check the flaps are neutral, set the propeller levers to the
maximum RPM position and the air intakes to cold, switch off
the master cocks, switch the pumps in No. 2 tanks on and
select No. 2 tanks, select the master cock required, switch on

the ignition and booster coil and then prime the engine.

They were now ready to start the engines. For engine starting, an external battery was used because of the high current consumption of the electrical starter motor situated on the starboard side of the engine. Mike Beetham pressed the starter button and, one by one, the engines roared into life. Each engine provided a drive to its propeller unit as well as individual drives to other services, including the hydraulic pumps to power each of the aircraft's gun turrets. Two twelve-cylinder magnetos were situated at the front of each engine, although only the starting magneto was boosted. The engine controls consisted of throttle controls and mixture controls. There were also engine supercharger controls and radiator shutter controls. A twin-choke carburettor supplied the correct fuel/air mixture to the supercharger on each engine. Fuel was pumped to the carburettor and air was delivered through an intake situated on the lower engine cowling. An air intake for the engine radiator and oil cooler was situated on the underside of the front cowling. Oil was circulated to the engine by a single pressure pump and returned to the oil tank by two scavenge pumps. The engine was liquid-cooled with a mixture of 30 per cent ethylene glycol and 70 per cent water.

When starting the engines it was the duty of the flight engineer, Don Moore, to monitor the oil pressures. Once all four Merlins had started the next thing was to check the engine temperatures and pressures, switch the ground/flight switch to 'flight', switch off the booster coil, test the hydraulic services by operating the bomb doors and flaps and once the coolant temperatures were correct, place the radiator override switches down. Everything was checked and then checked again. With more experience this would all come as second nature but, for now at least, time was in their hands.

Once airborne, the crew soon settled down. The Lancaster's main cockpit was spacious and the large canopy gave the front crew good all-round visibility. Mike Beetham was on the port side on a raised floor and the back of his seat was armour-plated. His main instrument panel was directly in front of him, the compass was situated by his left knee with a distant reading (DR) compass repeater on top of the front panel in the central position.

The responsibility for monitoring the engine instruments and aircraft systems were shared between the pilot and the flight engineer. Don Moore sat on a hinged seat on the starboard side of the main cockpit, where in the earlier days the second pilot used to sit. His responsibility was generally to assist the pilot from engine start through to final shut-down at the end of the sortie. He would also operate the aircraft's services such as flaps, undercarriage, throttle and propeller settings. To assist with monitoring the engines, the flight engineer's panel was located on the starboard side of the aircraft. It included engine oil temperature, coolant temperature and pressure gauges. One of Don Moore's main tasks was the management of the fuel system, which was critical should fuel have to be transferred between tanks in the event that the aircraft was hit. The total amount of fuel normally carried by the Lancaster was 2,154 gallons: 580 in each inboard wing tank, 383 in each intermediate wing tank and 114 in each outboard wing tank. When not carrying out any of his tasks, the flight engineer proved to be a valuable extra pair of eyes in the cockpit. He was also capable of flying the aircraft in the event of a major emergency; long enough, at least, for the crew to abandon the aircraft if necessary. Between the pilot and flight engineer was a central pedestal which housed the engine throttles and propeller controls within easy reach of both men. To improve the all-round visibility, the canopy had wide-view blisters on either side, which meant that the pilot and flight engineer could both see downwards.

The navigator, Frank Swinyard, sat at his plotting table on the port side of the main cockpit aft of the pilot's position. The navigation equipment in the Lancaster varied according to the mark of the aircraft and the layout even varied with the batch number. Essentially, the navigator's equipment consisted of repeaters of the main aircraft instruments:

compass, altimeter and airspeed indicator. Next to these was the air position indicator (API), which displayed in latitude and longitude the aircraft's position in still-air conditions without taking the wind velocity into account. The API was fed information from the aircraft's compass, the airspeed indicator and the altimeter. The aircraft's position was displayed to the navigator in four windows, which gave the north-south-east-west position. By calculating the wind velocity the navigator could work out the aircraft's track across the ground; this was particularly important during the final run in to the target.

The desire to equip Bomber Command's aircraft with accurate navigation equipment had been given great impetus in 1941. When the first Lancasters entered operational service in early 1942 only a few aircraft were fitted with Gee, an electronic navigation aid that gave the navigator a fix of the aircraft's position over the ground through the reception of signals from a series of ground stations. The original intention was for Gee-equipped Lancasters to lead raids within the operating range of the equipment, although this restricted the choice of targets for which it could be used. The system worked on line-of-sight and therefore depended on the aircraft's altitude. With favourable circumstances a maximum range of 400 miles was possible but more typically strong signals could be received out to about 150 miles, after which the signal strength reduced. Although Gee meant that most crews had little trouble finding the target area, the accuracy of the system varied and the aircraft's position could typically only be plotted within 5 miles.

More accurate navigation and bombing techniques were necessary and one of the many devices being considered was the use of an airborne radar system. The principle of airborne radar had been proved by Air-Surface Vessel (ASV) and Airborne Intercept (AI) devices, and there was no technical reason why a reasonable ground image should not be possible. The theory of the new airborne radar, H2S, was relatively straightforward. Pulses from the aircraft's transmitter travelled in straight lines and were reflected back from suitable surfaces. By displaying the returned pulses on a cathode ray tube, known as the plan position indicator (PPI), the returned pulses appeared in their relative position from the aircraft. Trials were conducted using Halifaxes equipped with a rotating scanner to give 360 degrees of cover and the system was first used operationally against Hamburg on the night of 30/31 January 1943.

Fitted to the Lancaster, the H2S scanner fairing is easily identified as a large blister situated on the underside of the rear fuselage, directly beneath the position of the mid-upper turret. The set inside the aircraft was situated at the navigator's station. There were problems to overcome, such as the stabilization of the picture during aircraft manoeuvre and the discrimination of pertinent features from the general ground clutter, but in practice H2S proved an excellent navigation aid as it provided good contrast between land and water. Coastal features, lakes and rivers were easy to identify and so general navigation, and hence aircraft position, proved fairly straightforward. Quite simply, H2S gave the navigator a picture of the ground ahead and beneath the aircraft, even at night or in cloudy weather, although its use was limited in extreme weather conditions. The navigator could identify a point on the ground and, by plotting a reciprocal relative bearing and distance from that point, he could obtain a fix. Also, by maintaining an air plot he could keep an accurate assessment of the wind velocity.

Although an excellent navigation aid, the employment of H2S as a bombing aid proved more problematical as it was often difficult to make out an accurate aiming point unless ground features were unique and distinguishable. To help the navigator, predictions and overlays were used to analyse the picture and interpret the radar picture but it took experience to make sense of the mass of radar returns. Cities near coastlines, such as Hamburg and Bremen, proved easier to cope with but large cities such as Berlin made the identification of aiming points more difficult.

By the end of 1943 about 90 per cent of Bomber Command aircraft were equipped with H2S and it was the most widely used navigation and bomb-aiming aid throughout the latter period of the war. During normal navigation the PPI showed the position of the aircraft in the centre but for blind bombing the radar picture was frozen with the target shown in the centre of the display and the aircraft off-set. The aircraft's heading and track were also displayed and, with the computer using the same information as required for visual bombing, a bombing marker was displayed on the PPI. The aircraft was then manoeuvred to keep the target marker under the track marker, and the bomb aimer would release the bomb load when the bombing marker, track marker and target marker all met together. This method was modified slightly if the target was not identified on radar. In this case, an identifiable point close to the target was used as an off-set, with its range and bearing from the target measured, and the aircraft would then be flown to the target marker using the same procedure as before.

Despite its limitations as an aid for blind bombing, due mainly to the problems caused by ground clutter, it would have been very difficult for crews to achieve any degree of accuracy without it. H2S also allowed Bomber Command to carry out operations in weather conditions that were unfavourable to normal visual bombing techniques. However, it did not take the Germans long to listen out for the H2S transmissions and thus discover the position of the bomber. The introduction of Naxos, a device used by the German night-fighters for homing in on H2S transmissions, led to crews becoming cautious and restrictions in the use of H2S over enemy territory were introduced.

Responsibility for communications and equipment, the electronic warfare equipment, and the authentication of codes and messages lay with the wireless operator, Reg Payne. His station inside the aircraft was at the back of the main cockpit adjacent to the leading edge of the wing. Like the navigation equipment, the wireless operator's equipment varied according to the mark and batch number of the Lancaster and also depended on what additional modifications had been fitted; this particularly applied to the electronic warfare equipment during the latter half of the war as more advanced technology was introduced. Essentially, Reg's main equipment was the radio installation and receiver, the ARI 5033, for which the aerial mast was located on top of the main canopy. He also had the direction-finding (DF) equipment, with the loop aerial also situated on top of the canopy, and the identification friend or foe (IFF) equipment.

The wireless operator was also generally responsible for checking the safety and survival equipment, such as the fire extinguisher, axe and signal pistol, because he was the crew member nearest to the equipment stowed in the centre section of the fuselage. Further aft was the release cable for the Type J dinghy, which was located in the root of the starboard wing, with a second release cable between the mid-upper turret and the tail. There was more safety equipment towards the rear of the aircraft. The safety and survival equipment for the Lancaster was good but there was always a problem abandoning the aircraft at night.

An analysis of bomber losses shows that fewer than 20 per cent of Lancaster crews survived being shot down, compared to the Halifax, where survival chances were nearly doubled. Looking at the Lancaster crew in very general terms, those in the front of the aircraft stood a better chance of abandoning the aircraft than those at the rear; statistically, about 10 per cent of Lancaster rear gunners survived compared to 30 per cent of Halifax rear gunners, and 20 per cent of Lancaster wireless operators survived compared to 40 per cent of Halifax wireless operators. It is also worth noting that survival rates amongst American bomber crews operating by day were even more favourable at about 50 per cent overall, which highlights the problem of operating at night when it became harder to find the escape hatches in the dark.

There were a number of escape hatches in the Lancaster: the cabin escape hatch in the top of the canopy, two emergency roof exits and the rear door. However, none of these was considered suitable for abandoning the aircraft by parachute. The Lancaster's flight engineer's notes state that the only official escape hatch for abandoning the aircraft was the forward one in the nose of the aircraft. The notes state that the use of the rear door was not recommended because of the close proximity to the tail section and it should only be used in the cases of extreme emergency; this was not the case in the Halifax, where the rear door was situated further forward. Needless to say, the rear door was used by many Lancaster crew members in cases of extreme emergency as the chances of the rear gunner, for example, making his way down the entire length of a burning aircraft, out of control at night, were almost zero.

Although the chances of successfully abandoning the Lancaster were statistically less than the Halifax, it should be remembered that Lancaster losses were proportionally fewer than the Halifax, and Bomber Command losses at night were less than those of American bombers by day. There were also several examples where the only member of a Lancaster crew to survive was the rear gunner and so there was no sure way of determining the chances of survival for any one crew position in any particular type of aircraft; there was an element of luck in surviving a tour of operations.

During take-off and landing the bomb aimer was supposed to be in the main cockpit but many stayed in the nose of the aircraft throughout the sortie. After take-off Les found his way to the bomb aimer's position in the nose of the aircraft. His view from the front was probably better than from any other bomber in service at the time. The lower part of the perspex blister incorporated an optically flat vision panel, which prevented any distortion when carrying out the final bombing run. His parachute was stowed on the left side of the nose compartment and his escape hatch was in the floor directly below his normal operating position. Aft of the bomb aimer's panel was a cockpit fire extinguisher and beneath the main panel was an additional small panel for the release of photo-flares. On the port side of the nose compartment, looking downward, was the F.24 camera installation.

The bomb aimer's panel was situated on the forward side of the nose and contained all the equipment that Les needed to carry out his task. In the top left-hand corner were sixteen bomb selector switches. Below these was the timing device used for stick-bombing with a dial that was set for the interval between bombs. The bomb aimer could also select the order in which the bombs were released to ensure that the aircraft's centre of gravity remained reasonably balanced as the bomb bay emptied: with several thousands of pounds of bombs spread along the bomb bay, which was 33 ft in length, it was essential that there was no great imbalance during the most vital part of the sortie. The panel also included the master switch, camera controls and heater switch to ensure that there was no hang-up of bombs at the point of release due to icing or freezing of the mechanism. Finally, the bomb release 'tit' held by the bomb aimer during the final run-in to the target had a stowed position on the panel with a guard to prevent an inadvertent operation.

The bomb aimer's main equipment consisted of a bomb sight and the panel just described. The standard sight of that period was the course-setting bomb sight (CSBS), which required a straight and level approach to the target prior to releasing the bomb load. Because the CSBS had been designed for daytime operations, its effectiveness at night was extremely limited and impractical over heavily defended targets. A more suitable sight was required for night operations, which would not rely on the pilot having to fly straight and level for any length of time over the target area. In addition, the number of bombers being used on raids was increasing and it was important for the bomber to spend as little time as possible over the target area. Furthermore, although CSBS was adequate for bombing cities and towns, it was not accurate enough for smaller targets such as railway junctions or individual buildings.

The replacement for the CSBS was the Mk XIV bomb sight,

which was more automated and stabilized, and proved far easier to operate; for example, the sight was not affected by aircraft manoeuvre. The system actually predicted where the bombs would land at any precise moment. To use the sight the bomb aimer looked through a reflector at a graticule which appeared to him to be on the ground, and the target moved along the graticule until it passed through the bomb-release line. The sight still relied on inputs from the bomb aimer to make sure that the correct bombing solution was displayed after taking into account all factors when bombing from high altitude. Some of these factors were fixed and could be pre-set during the sortie: for example, the target height above sea level, the regional air pressure in the target area, the weight of the aircraft and the terminal velocity of the bombs. The only real variable about the final bombing solution, and it was the most important, was the wind velocity, which was calculated and passed to the bomb aimer by the navigator. With all information entered into the computer, and with the height and air speed fed automatically into it, the final bombing solution was calculated and displayed. Needless to say, any errors inserted into the computer by the bomb aimer, such as an inaccurate wind velocity, led to errors in the final bombing solution. The computer was also designed to be used with the H2S radar for blind bombing, which meant that the target had to be identified on radar and a target marker placed over the target's radar return.

On operations Les would have the additional task of manning the hydraulically operated Nash and Thompson FN5A front turret during the long transits to and from the target area. The armament comprised two 0.303in Browning machine guns, with 1,000 rounds per gun of ammunition fed from boxes either side of him. His field of fire was 190 degrees traversal, sixty degrees in elevation and forty-five degrees in depression. Access to the turret was through doors which closed behind the gunner once in position. The turret was hydraulically powered, and could rotate at up to 90 degrees per second, but could also be rotated by hand in the event of a hydraulic failure.

Fred Ball was the 'tail-end Charlie' in the rear turret. The Nash and Thompson FN20 was the standard tail turret and had been developed from the FN4 fitted to the Manchester. Fred had four 0.303in Browning machine guns and his field of fire was 94 degrees to either beam, 60 degrees in elevation and 45 in depression. The ammunition was 2,500 rounds per gun, which was fed from the ammunition boxes in the rear fuselage, along ammunition belts. Entrance to the turret was through sliding doors, which were closed once the gunner was in position. Fred's only protection was three armoured plates beneath him. The turret was hydraulically powered but could also be hand operated in the event of a hydraulic failure. To abandon the aircraft from the turret, Fred would have to open the doors, grab his parachute from its stowage position just inside the rear fuselage, clip it on, traverse the turret to its full beam position, release himself from the seat harness and fall backwards away from the aircraft; not an easy task in the dark and extremely cold conditions with the aircraft, perhaps, tumbling out of control.

The mid-upper turret was the Nash and Thompson FN50, which was home to Jock Higgins. This turret was developed from the FN5 front turret and its armament was two 0.303in Browning machine guns, with 1,000 rounds per gun fed from two ammunition boxes either side of the gunner. Jock's field of fire was a full 360 degrees traversal, 20 degrees in elevation and just 2 degrees in depression. Access to the turret was from the top of the bomb bay on to a step and up into the turret in a standing position. Again, the turret was hydraulically powered but could be operated manually in the event of hydraulic failure. Jock's protection was provided by an armoured apron around the front of the turret, which protected him from the waist down. The all-round view from the mid-upper turret was excellent and was also quite good when looking vertically down. Although there was a reasonable amount of room in the turret, getting into it in full flying clothing proved cumbersome; getting out in an emergency would prove even harder, particularly if the aircraft was out of control.

Before Les knew it, they were coming in to land; their first crew solo sortie had lasted for just thirty-five minutes. Later in the day the crew flew their next sortie: more circuits, again lasting thirty-five minutes. By the end of the day they were all tired but there was still time for a drink or two to celebrate their successful day.

The crew was now let off the airfield 'lead' and the intensity of the flying increased; they could now expect to fly every day, and sometimes more than once. For example, on 4 October the crew flew one cross-country and air gunnery exercise during the day, followed by their first night-flying experience in the Lancaster. The first night sortie was dual familiarization, which lasted two hours and forty-five minutes, followed by a night solo sortie in the local circuit lasting forty minutes. It was a long and hard, but very rewarding, day for the crew; three training sorties totalling more than six hours airborne, three and a half of which had been at night.

When off duty the crew either spent the evening at the local pub in North Scarle or they ventured into Lincoln. Les was fortunate that Margaret was able to join him for a week when a local family in the village of North Scarle kindly put her up so that she could spend some time with Les. Time together was indeed precious. Both were aware that it would not be long before Les was on operations, with the obvious risks that would bring. Margaret was still working back at home and for Les there was so much to learn. The experience he had gained earlier in his training had prepared him well but now, all of a sudden, his tour of operations was only just a couple of weeks away and it was a steep learning curve for all of the crew.

Les had to learn not only about his new equipment but also about the different types of bomb carried by the Lancaster and the various bombing techniques and tactics employed by

Bomber Command. When the Lancaster first entered service the standard bombs were the 250lb and 500lb general purpose (GP) bombs, which were used for area bombing of non-hardened targets; there were hard points in the Lancaster bomb bay for at least eighteen of these smaller bombs to be carried.

With the introduction of the heavy bombers, the 1,000lb high-explosive bomb was developed for bombing of targets such as industrial areas and rail yards. The fusing was either nose-armed or tail-armed and was either instantaneous or delayed; the delayed fuse, in particular, gave the Germans a severe problem as it made the target area extremely hazardous long after the raid had taken place.

Although GP bombs were suitable for area bombing of towns and cities, more specialized weapons were needed against hardened targets. This led to the development of a range of semi-armour piercing (SAP) and armour-piercing (AP) bombs. During the early years of the war these were available as 250lb or 500lb SAP bombs but it was not long before a 2,000lb AP bomb was available for operations. An example of the employment of this new weapon was against the German battle cruiser *Gneisenau* docked at Kiel on the night of 26/27 February 1942 when a direct hit on the bow caused severe damage and killed more than 100 of its crew. The larger 4,000lb high capacity (HC) bomb, known as the 'Cookie', was developed during 1942 and appeared in various designs. The first version was designed with a cylindrical, mild steel casing filled with high explosive and a conical nose fitted with either an impact or a delayed fuse. The bomb contained amatol, minol or tritonal and was used for area bombing of tactical targets such as the V-weapons sites and larger industrial targets.

On the night of 4/5 February 1943 a new version of the weapon was dropped against the Italian port of La Spezia, using a proximity fuse. It exploded 500ft above the ground to widen the effects of the blast, although this version does not seem to have been widely used by Bomber Command. The success of the 4,000lb 'Cookie' led to a similarly shaped, but much larger weapon, the 8,000lb HC demolition bomb. It was, quite simply, two 4,000lb 'Cookies' joined end to end, and contained over 5,000lb of Amatex. It was designed for use against large and heavily defended industrial targets. Only one could be carried at a time and the bomb doors of the Lancaster had to be modified.

The middle period of the war saw the Germans build hardened U-boat pens and hardened launch sites for their new V-weapons. These hardened areas used reinforced concrete, which meant that Bomber Command required more specialized weapons if bombing was to have any success. Barnes Wallis, designer of the special Upkeep bomb used on the famous Dams Raid on the night of 16/17 May 1943, had spent much time working on a weapon for use against such targets. He calculated that a very strong, streamlined bomb dropped from high altitude would gain sufficient velocity to enable it to penetrate reinforced concrete before detonating. This led to the development of the first of the really large bombs to be carried by the Lancaster, the 12,000lb HC and the 12,000lb 'Tallboy'. The HC variant was similar in principle to the 4,000lb and 8,000lb HC bombs, although the 12,000lb variant needed fins. The first of these were dropped on the Dortmund–Ems Canal by Lancasters of No. 617 Sqn on the night of 15/16 September 1943.

When the 'Tallboy' version entered service, it was the largest and heaviest bomb ever carried by an aircraft. This version was a spin-stabilized bomb, 21ft in length, and contained 6,000lb of Torpex D; the effect when dropped was to cause an earthquake in the target area. As with the other large weapons, only one bomb could be carried at any one time and required the aircraft to have modified bomb doors. These 12,000lb bombs were not to be the last of the big bombs and the largest, the 22,000lb 'Grand Slam' was still yet to come, although this monster weapon would not be used until just before the end of the war.

Bombing had come a long way during 1943 but bombing a

target at night, particularly in bad weather, remained a diffi-cult task. As a result Bomber Command had to develop new tactics and techniques during the course of the war. These included the improvement of marking a target at night, often in bad weather, when traditional visual bombing techniques were not possible. If a raid was to be successful then it was important to correctly identify the aiming point for the target; the combination of experienced crews and specialist equip-ment increased the chances of success.

To ensure that an aiming point was obvious to main force crews it was necessary to develop a method that made the aiming point clearly visible and one that stood out against the fires and any lights around the target area. Decoy fires were also started by the Germans on the ground to confuse the bomb aimers and any early release of bombs led to an overall 'creep back' by the main force. All this, and the amount of flak, led to general confusion in the target area.

The development of the target indicator (TI) during 1943 helped solve this problem. This was essentially a 250lb bomb case filled with sixty candles (green, red or yellow), which were dropped by the lead aircraft to mark the aiming point. At a height of 3,000ft a barometric fuse caused the candles to eject and then ignite before falling to the ground. This early method was ground marking a target but the early TIs only burnt for a few minutes, which was not long enough for a large main force of bombers. Therefore, longer burning candles were introduced, which also ignited at different inter-vals, so that the aiming point was marked over a longer period of time; the problem with this method was that fewer candles were burning at any one time, making the aiming point less bright and, therefore, less obvious. This led to larger TIs such as a 1,000lb bomb case with 200 candles, which meant that a much larger area could be lit for about twenty minutes.

Unsurprisingly the ground markers could be put out and the Germans soon learned to use decoy TIs. One counter to this was for the bombers to drop exploding candles, which gave the German fire services a considerable problem when attempting to extinguish fires on the ground. So the TI and counter-TI war went on. Ground marking was carried out either visually or blind; the visual method was known as Newhaven and the blind method as Parramatta. Newhaven involved flares being dropped by 'illuminator' aircraft followed by the 'visual markers' with the task of using the light of the flares to identify the aiming point and then drop the TIs in the right place. This method was further developed during 1944 by including a master bomber to assess where the best TIs were, and then to broadcast information to the main force; this was Musical Newhaven.

The main problem with ground marking was that the method relied on good weather in the target area; any cloud simply prevented the main force bomb aimers seeing the aiming point. Parramatta was used when visual techniques could not be used. Lancasters using H2S identified the target and aiming point, and then the TIs were dropped blind. When Oboe was later developed and used, instead of H2S, the method became known as Musical Parramatta. The introduction of blind bombing techniques led to a method of sky marking, known as Wanganui, rather than ground marking. Sky markers were generally flares (although candles were still used on occasions), which were dropped either as singles or in groups. An air-burst fuse ejected the flare from its container. It would then ignite and a parachute would deploy so that the flare dropped slowly to the ground. Later modifications used larger bomb cases, either 500lb or 1,000lb, which ejected flares of different colours and at various intervals to produce a 'ladder' effect. Assuming little or no wind, the Main Force simply bombed the flares above the cloud.

To help assess the results of bombing raids, it was necessary to develop good photographic techniques. One problem during the early years of the war was the paucity of cameras. In 1941, for example, there were only about four night-capable cameras per squadron. There were also the obvious problems with night photography, such as cloud and haze. In the Lancaster, the camera started operating when the bomb aimer released the bombs and continued until the calculated moment of impact. The open-plate camera took a series of pictures during the time that it was exposed, with the light being provided by the photoflash and any additional lighting in the area, such as the TIs, searchlights and flak. The fact that the camera continued to operate until the point of impact meant that the aircraft had to remain straight and level over the target area for a further thirty seconds or so; not surprisingly this was something that many bomber crews were reluctant to do!

Having learned all about weapons and bombing techniques, there were two training sorties on the HCU dedicated to learning how to survive when under threat. The Beetham crew flew the first sortie (combat manoeuvres) on 8 October and the second (fighter affiliation) the following day. Somewhat surprisingly, these were the only dedicated training sorties for the crew to learn how to survive when under threat from searchlights and flak or when under attack by an enemy night fighter. Considering that the likelihood of these situations arising for real was as certain as the sun rising every morning, the crew did not have much time in the air to gain any real handling experience, as the two sorties combined lasted for less than two hours. The crew would often discuss what they would do when the situation arose for the first time for real but it soon became obvious to each of them that they would have to learn fast, or not survive at all.

The bomber crew truly relied on each other for their lives and no one could afford to let the side down. Of course, when under attack for real, much would depend on the aircraft-handling skills of the pilot, Mike Beetham. He had to learn the Lancaster's standard defensive manoeuvre when under attack from a fighter, known as the 'corkscrew'. Assuming an attack from the port side, the manoeuvre was: a steep dive to port; followed by a roll over and climb to starboard. At the top of the climb, dive to starboard, roll over and climb to port.

The important thing was to lose as little height as possible during the manoeuvre. If the initial attack came from the starboard side then the first dive would be to starboard as the Lancaster should always turn initially into the attacker, the theory being that during the roll over the Lancaster passed through the fighter's gun sight so quickly that it was more difficult for the fighter pilot to get a sighting solution. Defensive manoeuvres were not at all comfortable for the rest of the crew. Les often found that in steep dives he would be pinned to the roof of the bomb aimer's compartment through zero gravity with his maps and instruments all over the place.

The crew's next two training sorties were both flown at night. The first, on the evening of 17 October, was a cross-country navigation exercise followed by high level bombing practice, and lasted more than three hours. The second was flown on the following evening and involved the crew working against searchlights and the night-fighter threat, and lasted three hours. The crew's last training sortie on the HCU was a daytime exercise flown on 20 October, a cross-country navigation exercise followed by daytime practice bombing, which lasted nearly six hours.

Although the crew had by then spent hours learning about the Lancaster and its specialist equipment, these training sorties gave them valuable time in the air to operate their equipment and get more used to their surroundings. Les had flown thirty hours on the HCU, bringing his total flying time (including his sixty-one hours' pilot training) to just over 200 hours. At the end of the HCU course, the Beetham crew was posted to No. 50 Sqn and they arrived at nearby RAF Skellingthorpe at the end of October 1943. As far as their training was concerned, that was it; there was to be no more. Everything that was to happen from now on was to be for real.

CHAPTER FOUR

The Big City

Compared to other European cities, Berlin might be considered relatively young. The origins of the historic city date back to the early thirteenth century, when it was part of German expansion east of the River Elbe. The two founding towns, Kölln and Berlin, affiliated in 1307 and Friedrich II later declared the twin towns as his residence in 1451. In 1701 Friedrich III declared himself as King Friedrich I of Prussia and Berlin rose to become the royal capital. This led to the architectural redesign of the city and many famous buildings soon appeared. During its more recent history, the industrial revolution of the nineteenth century had transformed it and led to its economy and population expanding dramatically. Berlin soon became the main rail hub and economic centre of Germany and, in 1871, became capital of the newly founded German Empire. At the end of the First World War the Weimar Republic was proclaimed in Berlin and it was not long before all the suburban areas around the city had been brought into Berlin's administration, bringing the capital's population to about four million people.

With the rise of Adolf Hitler and his National Socialists during 1933 Berlin became the capital of the Third Reich and the Reichstag became the centre of Hitler's power. Berlin was, and still is, a large city by any standards. Not only was it Germany's largest city by some considerable margin, but it was the third largest city in the world. It measures about 25 miles north–south, and 30 miles east–west, and its total area is in the order of 390 square miles. The main city is centred on its five central districts: Tiergarten, with its marvellous zoological garden and famous landmarks of the Reichstag, the Victory Column and the Brandenburg Gate; Mitte; Kreuzberg; Wilmersdorf, where the Kaiser Wilhelm Church is located; and Charlottenburg, site of the famous Schloss Charlottenburg commissioned by Queen Sophie Charlotte in 1695. Surrounding the central districts are many more districts, including: Wedding and Reinickendorf to the north, Spandau to the west, Zehlendorf to the south-west, Steglitz and Tempelhof to the south, Neukölln, Treptow and Köpenick to the south-east, Friedrichshain and Lichtenberg to the east; and Prenzlauerberg and Weissensee to the north-east. To the west of the city, running from the north-west to the south-west, is a line of forests and lakes.

Being at the centre of Nazi Germany, Berlin was understandably the 'big one' when it came to Bomber Command's key targets. This was not only because of what the city represented but also because of its factories and communications links, as well as its geographical position lying midway between the Western and Eastern Fronts. Because Berlin was situated so deep into Germany it had hardly been touched during the early years of the war. There had been a retaliatory raid by Bomber Command during the Battle of Britain on the night of 25/26 August 1940. This was not a particularly concentrated effort but was one of a number of small-scale raids against various targets in Germany during the night. For the fifty or so Hampden and Wellington crews that took part, it was a monumental effort as Berlin was at the maximum range of the Hampden. Conditions were not ideal as a strong head-wind on the return leg caused some of the Hampdens to ditch in the sea. Although the raid was not particularly successful, as the weather in the target area was cloudy and very few bombs fell inside the city boundary, it did demonstrate to the German people that the RAF was capable of reaching their capital, even in the early stages of the war.

Bomber Command's effort during the summer of 1940 was

generally small-scale as priority was understandably given to the squadrons of Fighter Command to ensure that Britain survived the *Luftwaffe*'s onslaught during the Battle of Britain. The raids that were possible were carried out by small numbers of bombers at night, with crews generally left to find their own way to the target and to do the best they could; both navigation and bombing techniques were basic to say the least and the fact that Bomber Command achieved any success was largely down to the professionalism and determination of the crews.

The first concentrated raid against Berlin was on the night of 23/24 September 1940. The reason for the timing of this raid is a little unclear as it came at a time when Bomber Command's efforts were mainly against the Channel ports in a bid to deter a German invasion of England. The attacking force was 129 aircraft and was made up of Hampdens, Wellingtons and Whitleys. There was no one specific target and the force bombed various targets in and around Berlin, mainly railway yards, factories and power stations. The results of this raid are unclear but, if nothing else, it would again have had an effect on the morale of the German people and made sure that German defences were spread across a wide area.

Once the threat of a German invasion of Britain had disappeared, for the time being at least, Bomber Command continued its offensive. Its commander-in-chief, Sir Charles Portal, left to take up the appointment as Chief of the Air Staff and was replaced by Air Marshal Sir Richard Peirse. Portal's deputy was Arthur Harris, who left his previous appointment as Air Officer Commanding (AOC) No. 5 Group. Although there were occasional raids against Berlin, the strategic offensive turned to attacking targets connected with the oil industry. The priority changed once more during early 1941 following German successes in the North Atlantic when Bomber Command turned its attention to shipbuilding yards and U-boats, with targets ranging from the ports to the factories producing the diesel engines. Bomber Command was unable to make much of an impact on the war in the Atlantic and so turned its attention back to Germany. Targets were mainly around the industrial area of the Ruhr but when this was not possible they included the major German cities. Berlin was included in this new phase and was attacked a number of times during the latter half of 1941.

The most notable of the 1941 raids against Berlin took place on the nights of 7/8 September and 7/8 November. The first of these was a mixed force of 197 bombers: Wellingtons, Hampdens, Whitleys, Stirlings, Halifaxes and Manchesters. Clear weather conditions led to two-thirds of the force bombing the city, which caused damage to factories, transportation and housing. The second involved a bombing force twice that of the September effort, although not all were despatched to Berlin. Of the 392 aircraft involved on operations on the night of 7/8 November, which marked a record number of Bomber Command sorties in one night, 169 took part in the raid on Berlin. These were Wellingtons, Whitleys, Stirlings and Halifaxes of Nos 1, 3 and 4 Groups but no aircraft from No 5. Group were involved. The forecast of bad weather *en route* to the target, particularly over the North Sea, led to the AOC No. 5 Group, Air Vice-Marshal John Slessor, cancelling his group's involvement in the raid. His force of Hampdens and Manchesters was sent to Cologne instead which, with hindsight, was probably a good decision as no aircraft were lost on the Cologne raid, although it must also be said that the raid did not cause any significant damage. Of the bombers that went to Berlin, fewer than half found the target area and damage to the city was slight. Twenty-one of the aircraft failed to return, which represents more than 12 per cent of the force dispatched. Operations that night also included a raid against Mannheim and minor operations in other areas. Of all the aircraft dispatched on operations that night, thirty-seven failed to return, just under 10 per cent of the total effort. It is believed that many of these losses were due to bad weather over the North Sea with many of the crews lost without trace, their aircraft having suffered from the effects of severe icing.

This was the last major effort against Berlin for more than a year. Whilst the decision to press on with operations on the night of 7/8 November 1941 might have cost Sir Richard Peirse his command, it would be wrong to single out one bad night, because the reality was that Bomber Command had suffered a run of poor results and high losses. Sir Richard Peirse was removed from his post as Commander-in-Chief in early January 1942 and later took command of the Allied Air Forces in India and South-East Asia. He was temporarily replaced by the AOC No. 3 Group, Air Vice-Marshal J. Baldwin, until the appointment of Arthur Harris on 22 February 1942.

When he took up his command, Harris inherited a force of fewer than 500 bombers, nearly half of which were Wellingtons, and a change in strategic policy, which would lead to area bombing of Germany's most densely populated areas. Although the bombing campaign was well into its third year, the equipment and techniques made accurate bombing of specific targets, such as industrial installations, difficult and results had not been particularly good. This is in no way a reflection on the efforts of the command and its crews but more on the aircraft and technology available at the time.

It has, perhaps, been wrongly suggested over the years that Arthur Harris was responsible for the strategy of area bombing of German cities but it was more the Chief of the Air Staff, Sir Charles Portal, and his staff at the Air Ministry that believed in the general area bombing of populated areas to spread defences and to defeat the morale of the German people. Interestingly, this method of warfare had not defeated the morale of London's citizens during the blitz but bombing large areas, such as cities, at night or in bad weather had more chance of success than bombing a specific factory or building. Portal had gained the support of the Prime Minister, Winston Churchill, and other senior officers, which led to the Air Ministry issuing the new directive to Bomber Command before Harris had taken up his appointment as the Commander-in-Chief. Harris certainly supported the policy and was given the responsibility of enforcing it; had he not done so then it is unlikely that he would have been appointed.

If Bomber Command was to succeed, it needed heavier bombers which were capable of reaching deeper into Germany and delivering a bomb load of significance, better equipment for navigation and bombing, and strong leadership. For Harris, the timing of his appointment was fortunate in that the first of the new four-engined bombers had just entered service and there were some significant advances in technology, particularly in the development of navigation equipment. However, the strong leadership required was to be purely down to his own style if he was to get the best out of his bomber crews.

Throughout 1942 there were significant efforts against Essen, Cologne, Lübeck, Dortmund, Hamburg, Mannheim, Bremen, Emden, Wilhelmshaven, Duisburg, Saarbrücken, Düsseldorf, Frankfurt, Kassel, Kiel and Stuttgart. These ranged from the huge Thousand Bomber raids to smaller-scale efforts, although Bomber Command's targets were not just restricted to Germany but also included a multitude of sites throughout occupied Europe. There were even raids against targets in Italy in support of the Eighth Army's campaign in North Africa, but there was nothing against Berlin during 1942.

One of the main reasons for this was because of the distance to Berlin, which increased exposure to ground defences and enemy fighters during the long transit to and from the target area, as well as making navigation over such a distance and then identifying the target a challenge to say the least. Another significant reason was that Bomber Command losses were steadily increasing; during the summer of 1942 the average losses went over the 4 per cent mark. This undoubtedly had an affect on the morale within the command and the risk of even higher losses, which would probably have been inevitable had Bomber Command returned to Berlin, was not considered worth taking.

Things would, however, soon improve. The addition of the

United States Eighth Air Force to the overall effort was to prove significant and the formation within Bomber Command of the new Pathfinder Force (PFF) in August 1942 would improve bombing techniques and the bombing results. Harris had initially resisted the idea of developing an elite force, preferring instead to maintain experience at the squadron level, but the formation of the PFF went a long way to solving the problem of identifying and marking targets. Each group provided one squadron to the PFF: No. 156 Sqn from No. 1 Group, No. 7 Sqn from No. 3 Group, No. 35 Sqn from No. 4 Group and No. 83 Sqn from No. 5 Group. Serving with the PFF was voluntary and, although it had initially been suggested that each squadron should ask its more experienced crews to 'volunteer', this did not always prove to be the case. The fact that each group had given one squadron did provide the force with the problem of operating four different types of aircraft: Lancasters, Halifaxes, Stirlings and Wellingtons. The PFF was given group status, as No. 8 Group, in January 1943 with Air Commodore Donald Bennett as its first commander.

By early 1943 Bomber Command's expansion and the introduction of the four-engined 'heavies' meant that the number of bombers available for a main effort had doubled, from 200 at the turn of the previous year to 400, as had the effective total bomb load against a target, which by 1943 was typically more than 2 tons against the closer targets. However, although things were improving for Bomber Command, the same could be said for the German defences and night-fighter capability. The war was not going well for Germany both on the Eastern Front and in North Africa and so thoughts had already turned to the defence of Germany and, in particular, the defence of what would be the biggest prize of all for the Allies – Berlin.

The main elements of the German defence organization were: ground control interception (GCI), searchlights, anti-aircraft artillery (flak) and, of course, night fighters. By 1943 all were inter-connected and formed an effective system that was already causing heavy casualties amongst Bomber Command's crews. The standard German radar was Freya, which had a maximum detection range of up to 180 miles. It proved to be a very good and accurate system but lacked a true height-finding capability. Two longer-range radars were developed, Chimney and Mammut, which increased detection ranges to 250 miles; this, of course, depended on the bomber's height.

The principle of the searchlights was to assist the anti-aircraft guns and night fighters. Most of the major targets in Germany, including Berlin, had extensive searchlight defences with dozens of beams lighting up the sky. In a coordinated system with sound locators, optical devices and radar, the master beam (usually distinguishable by its blue/mauve tinge) would latch on to a bomber, which would then be followed by many other searchlights forming a cone of light for the anti-aircraft batteries to focus on. The total number of searchlights doubled in Germany between 1941 and 1944 by which time there were nearly 5,000 in operation.

Anti-aircraft guns, or flak from *fliegerabwehrkanonen*, were divided into light and heavy. The light units were used for point defence of important targets. These units varied from 20mm to 50mm and were optically laid. The maximum rate of fire was over 200 rounds per minute. Although essentially used against bombers at lower altitudes, the light units were still effective at heights of 10,000ft or more. The heavy guns were usually used in batteries of four or six and tactics were either aimed fire, which relied on important data from a source such as radar, or unaimed box barrage. The heavy guns varied from 88mm to 128mm and had rates of fire up to twenty rounds per minute with maximum ranges varying up to 22,000 yards with a maximum ceiling of up to 40,000ft.

Around Berlin there were about 600 flak units, of which 350 were heavy, and 200 searchlights. In addition there were the German night-fighter defences, which had quickly evolved from a not particularly effective arrangement of single-engined Messerschmitt Bf109s to a complex organization that provided layer defence deep into the heart of Germany.

The increased use of radar meant that the bombers were picked up early and handed off to a controller for interception by the waiting night fighters. In essence the system evolved into two main types: *Wilde Sau* (Wild Boar), which was the re-introduction of the single-engined fighter to the night fighting role, and *Zähme Sau* (Tame Boar), which was an extension of the existing controlled tactic. The proposal of the *Wilde Sau* tactics by Major Hans-Joachim Hermann had proved particularly successful with the introduction of a specialist night-fighting unit, JG300, in the Bonn area, and this led to the formation of JG302 for the defence of Berlin. The introduction of *Schräge Musik* (Jazz Music), twin upward-firing cannon fitted to Messerschmitt Bf110s during 1943, led to the development of the most successful night-fighter tactic against Bomber Command, attacking from below and behind and then firing up into the belly of the bomber, often with devastating success. The bomber's answer was to keep manoeuvring and, if necessary, to 'corkscrew'; a manoeuvre which undoubtedly saved many bomber crews' lives. The night bombing war was a battle of wits, new tactics, new counters, revised tactics, revised counters, and so on.

Bomber Command returned to Berlin on the night of 16/17 January 1943. This was the first raid on the capital since November 1941 and the force of 200 bombers was essentially an all-Lancaster force with just eleven Halifaxes making up the numbers. Unfortunately, it was not a success. The weather *en route* to the target was not good, the bombers were operating beyond the range of the new Gee navigation aid and H2S had not yet been introduced into service. Bombing was spread across the southern districts of the city but there was no significant damage, although some 200 citizens were killed. Just one Lancaster failed to return. The weather was better on the following night as Bomber Command returned to Berlin once more. A similar-sized force took the same route to the capital, which led to the main stream being intercepted by German night fighters. More than twenty bombers failed to reach the target and those that did bombed the southern districts once more, again without causing any significant damage.

Although not particularly successful, these two raids at the start of the year were a sign of things to come for the population of Berlin. On 30 January two raids, one in the morning and one in the afternoon, each by just three Mosquitoes, disrupted key speeches being made by senior Nazis at large rallies. Although very small-scale, these raids were significant in that they were the first daylight raids against Berlin. One Mosquito taking part in the afternoon raid was shot down but it again showed that Bomber Command had the capability to attack Berlin whenever it wanted.

If the raid on 30 January had been small-scale, the next attack on Berlin was completely the opposite; it was the largest concentrated effort on the capital to date. On the night of 1/2 March more than 300 aircraft caused more damage to the city than had been achieved before. Although the raid was only partially successful in terms of the numbers of bombers that actually bombed the target and the accuracy they achieved, there was damage across a large area of the city, particularly in the south-western districts. This proved the point that large numbers of aircraft, with increased bomb loads, could cause considerable damage across a vast area of 100 square miles. Half of the attacking force was Lancasters, the other half being made up of Halifaxes and Stirlings. Unfortunately, losses were above the norm and above the rate that Bomber Command could sustain, seventeen aircraft failed to return (nearly 6 per cent of the force dispatched).

There were two further raids against Berlin in March 1943. Nearly 400 bombers took part in a disappointing raid on the night of 27/28 March when no bombs were recorded within 5 miles of the aiming point and all bombs dropped short of the intended target. Two nights later, on 29/30 March, more than 300 bombers were dispatched to Berlin in difficult weather conditions. Inaccurate wind calculations again led to the bombs falling too far south, and again losses were high, twenty-one aircraft lost (over 6 per cent of the force dispatched).

For the time being, at least, Berlin was now left alone as Bomber Command concentrated its main effort on industrial targets in what became known as the Battle of the Ruhr, and then the Battle of Hamburg, which was Germany's second largest city and boasted Europe's largest port. However, it had always been Harris's intent to return to Berlin but next time in a major offensive rather than small-scale isolated raids. There was an opportunity at the end of August 1943 and Harris dispatched three major raids in a period of two weeks at the end of the month and in early September.

The first was on the night of 23/24 August, and involved the largest number of aircraft sent to the capital to date, 727. Bombing was spread over a large area, mostly in the southern suburbs and outside the city. More than 800 people were killed on the ground, most of whom were civilians. Bomber Command losses were again high, due to strong anti-aircraft defences and night-fighter activity, with fifty-six aircraft failing to return (almost 8 per cent of the force dispatched). It was Bomber Command's highest number of aircraft lost in one night of the war to date.

The second raid in this series of three was on the night of 31 August/1 September when 622 aircraft were dispatched to the capital. Again the raid was not a success and again Bomber Command's losses were high due to the strong German defences; a further forty-seven aircraft (7.6 per cent of the force) failed to return. Losses were particularly high amongst the Halifaxes and Stirlings. Twenty of the 176 Halifaxes failed to return, as did seventeen of the 106 Stirlings.

The third raid took place on the night of 3/4 September and was an all-Lancaster effort but again the losses were high: twenty-two Lancasters from 316 dispatched. This time the raid approached from the north-east but the bombing fell mainly short, although there was damage to the industrial area in the western districts as well as to residential areas.

These three concentrated efforts in two weeks were effectively the start of the Battle of Berlin. However, they cost Bomber Command 125 aircraft and crews, significantly above the losses being sustained against other targets, and so the start of what was to become Bomber Command's major offensive of the war was postponed. Not only were losses high but bombing results were not as expected. Navigation and bombing techniques had improved to some extent but Berlin was simply beyond the range of the new navigation aids, Gee and Oboe, and the use of H2S was not proving as successful as had initially been hoped; although this was mainly due to Berlin's inland location rather than because of the equipment.

Harris again decided to leave Berlin alone until better equipment was more readily available and the long winter nights had set in; the scene was now set for the Battle of Berlin to commence in earnest. It was October 1943.

CHAPTER FIVE

Operations at Last

The airfield at RAF Skellingthorpe was located just 3 miles to the south-west of the city of Lincoln. Today the site has been developed as a large housing estate but in October 1943, when Les and his crew commenced their tour of operations, it was an active bomber airfield within No. 5 Group of Bomber Command. It was one of the command's newest airfields, having been opened just two years earlier as a satellite airfield for nearby Swinderby. It had been developed on grass fields, surrounded by gravel pits, woods and a lake.

No. 50 Sqn was the first unit to operate from the airfield when it moved its Hampdens in from Swinderby during November 1941. The squadron briefly converted to the Manchester during May 1942 and during the following month moved back to Swinderby so that the airfield at Skellingthorpe could be prepared for the introduction of Lancasters. Having converted to the Lancaster, and with work at Skellingthorpe all but complete, No. 50 Sqn returned in October 1942 and remained there for the rest of the war.

The construction at Skellingthorpe was part of Britain's major construction programme of 1942. It was the largest construction programme since the expansion scheme of the mid-1930s, and the arrival of the United States Army Air Force (USAAF) during 1942 added to the number of airfields needed. The grass runways were replaced by three standard wartime concrete runways, intersecting and linked by a perimeter track. The main one was about 2,000 yards in length and 50 yards wide, and ran from the south-west corner of the airfield to the north-east, which gave the crews a good view of Lincoln Cathedral when taking off in that direction; the two others were shorter, about 1,400 yards long.

The perimeter track around the airfield was 50ft wide and the introduction of the Lancaster heavy bomber meant that aircraft dispersal points were constructed around the perimeter track with facilities for two squadrons. These dispersals areas were where all routine servicing was carried out and, had to be strong enough to support a fully laden Lancaster.

The Beetham crew arrived at Skellingthorpe on 26 October 1943 for their tour of operations. At that time, No. 50 Sqn was commanded by Wing Commander Robert McFarlane, who had taken over in August. Born in Glasgow in 1914, he had quickly gained a good reputation within Bomber Command and he very quickly earned the respect of his squadron. He had already been decorated with the Distinguished Flying Cross (DFC) and bar, the second of which followed his heroic attack on the German battle cruisers *Scharnhorst* and *Gneisenau* in the English Channel the previous year, and he would soon add the Distinguished Service Order (DSO) to his decorations.

On arrival the crew were immediately shown to their accommodation, the officers to the officers' mess and the sergeants to their Nissen hut. It was a cold and damp evening. The sergeants started to settle in and soon met up with one of the other squadron members. At a loss for something to do, they were told that the centre of Lincoln was just fifteen minutes away by bicycle and that they would soon find everything they were looking for. Without waiting a minute longer, Les, Reg Payne and Fred Ball were soon pedalling their way into Lincoln.

The pubs were hard to find in the blackout but one, The Unity, was eventually spotted as someone opened the door to leave. Inside, they sampled the local beer and soon got chatting to a couple of Auxiliary Territorial Service (ATS) girls.

When it was time to leave, Reg and Fred offered to walk the girls back to their quarters a short distance away and so began a long relationship between the two young RAF sergeants and the two young ATS girls during their time at Skellingthorpe. For one couple, Reg and Ena, it was the start of a lifelong relationship as they were to be married in 1945; the couple would spend forty-three happily married years together until Ena sadly died in 1988.

It is now time to include extracts from the diary that Les kept throughout his tour of operations; they are reproduced as Les recorded them at the time:

Tuesday 26 October 1943

At long last we are now on an operational squadron, one of the best in 5 Group, or so we are told. So this is where the 'Big Shows' go on; it seems difficult to believe. Everything was so quiet and peaceful and hardly anyone was to be seen; obviously there are no operations tonight. Our first stop was the mess, naturally, that's the most important place on any station, it was a pleasant surprise too, after some of those places in Training Command in which we have 'existed'. I'm afraid our quarters could have been better, to live in a Nissen hut in the middle of winter in Lincolnshire isn't exactly ideal however, we are sharing it with another crew so we have company if nothing else. They're jolly decent blokes but can't give us any 'gen' having only arrived themselves two days ago! It's good to think we aren't the only 'sprogs' on the squadron.

Wednesday 27 October

At 0930 hrs we went up to the 'drome to put in an appearance at the flight offices and signed in at our respective sections. Seems a pretty easy going place and everyone is keen to give us all the 'gen'. Next stop was the stores where we drew electrically heated flying suits, gloves and socks, also the latest in flying boots 'escape type'. There was a knife in a small inside pocket of the boot. If you were shot down you could use it to cut off the lamb's wool sides of your flying boots leaving you with a pair of ordinary looking boots.

Thursday 28 October

This morning we were told that our aircraft was to be 'A-Able' in 'A' flight, so off we went to look it over. Oh! What a beauty, so clean you could eat your breakfast from the floor, and tidy too, different from our last kite at Con Unit, which was a shambles – you couldn't help tripping over dinghies and flame floats, sliding on empty cartridge cases and slipping in oil which seemed to leak from everywhere. This is different. 'A-Able' has got all the latest modifications known to science, so the sooner we get airborne and bombing the better.

Saturday 30 October

Bags of panic! 'Ops' tonight and Mike our pilot is doing his 'second dickey' trip in 'A-Able' with Flt/Lt Boulton and crew (veterans with twenty-three major operations to their credit). At 1800 hrs 'ops' were scrubbed due to 'duff' weather coming in, so F/O Beetham and crew went to town for a drink – 'nuff' said.

The crew that Mike Beetham flew with on that occasion were shot down soon after during a raid against Berlin on the night of 2/3 December. Flight Lieutenant Boulton and four of his crew members were taken as prisoners of war, as was a war correspondent from the *Daily Express*, who was flying with the crew at the time; sadly the bomb aimer and mid-upper air gunner were both killed.

Les and his crew colleagues quickly settled down to life on

a Bomber Command station. His diary records his first few days at Skellingthorpe.

It was late autumn, dull, wet and with lots of mud about. We NCOs in the crew were billeted in a Nissen hut containing ten beds and the traditional iron coke stove in the centre. There were five of us and we shared the hut with the NCOs of another crew. After checking in, it was time to get acquainted with the station and to find out where everything was located. The sergeants' mess – what was the food like? Where was the NAAFI? Is there a cinema? What was discipline like and were the SPs [RAF Service Police] human? All these things helped to make life on a Bomber station tolerable.

After duty we were free to do a 'recce' so we mounted our issue bikes and proceeded to explore the adjacent countryside. In a nearby village called North Scarle we found two pubs, one of which, The Sedan Chair, looked inviting so in we went. It was quaint but cosy and we soon felt at home. The landlady 'took to' us and I got the feeling that she would be mothering the younger members of the crew. This turned out to be to their advantage, getting washing done etc. After a few beers we departed, and further down the High Street we saw a tree absolutely laden with lovely red apples. There was a low wall between the apples and us and Reg, our wireless operator, was all for scaling the wall and helping ourselves – 'scrumping' it was called. However, I dissuaded him and suggested the correct thing to do was to go to the farmhouse, knock on the door and ask if they would sell us some apples. To make sure Reg did the right thing I escorted him to the door and of course they gave us as many apples as we could carry away. The farm was Holme Farm; the family was Mr and Mrs Dixon with son Wilf and daughter Stella. I returned subsequently to ask if I could buy eggs from them. On the station, as everywhere in the UK, the nearest you got to an egg was the powdered variety which was 'yuck', but with a little persuasion the WAAFs in the mess would take your eggs and cook them for you – at a price. At first an extra egg was the price then the price got higher! When we settled in we discovered that when on operations you always had a meal including a fried egg before operations and again on your return – if you returned – you had another egg with your breakfast.

The outcome of the apple episode was that Les and his colleagues became great friends of the farmer and his family and they were often invited to have a meal with them when off duty. Les spent much of his spare time when off duty driving the farm tractor when they needed help. Haymaking was great fun; the family brought picnic baskets to the fields and to Les the food was out of this world compared with service rations on the station.

Wednesday 3 November

What a day I've had. 'Ops' tonight – but not for our crew, so I went and helped the armourers with 'bombing-up' the kites. Gee! – I've never worked so hard in all my life, it's no piece of cake winding the winches with a 4,000lb bomb on the end of the cables, it took us an hour to do each kite and the ground crew of the last kite were already running up the engines before we had finished. At 1720 hrs we went to watch take-off. It was broad daylight and a lovely sight, all tearing round the sky waiting for time to set course. At 0230 hrs the squadron was back on the deck without loss and the German radio could be saying, 'One of our cities is missing' – Düsseldorf.

Bomber Command records show that this raid by nearly 600 heavy bombers against Düsseldorf was successful in that there was extensive damage to the city, although it is difficult to determine how much damage was caused to the industrial targets. Eighteen aircraft failed to return (3 per cent of the force dispatched). The raid also marked the first large-scale use of AR.5525, known as 'G-H', as a blind-bombing aid against a tubular steels works on the northern side of the city. Thirty-eight Lancasters were fitted with G-H but for various reasons only fifteen were able to bomb the target using the system.

The system was not entirely new, as it had been proposed at the same time as Gee was being developed. It would in theory have been more accurate than Gee but, like Oboe, would be limited in the number of aircraft that could use it at any one time. The system effectively worked in the opposite way to Oboe in that the aircraft transmitted to mobile stations to get its information for fixes. The system relied on the aircrew for accuracy but G-H did become an extremely capable blind-bombing aid. Lancasters fitted with it often had their fins painted in different colours, which made them easy to identify so that other aircraft could follow them in to the target.

The raid against Düsseldorf on the night of 3/4 November also saw the award of the Victoria Cross to Flight Lieutenant Bill Reid of No. 61 Sqn for his outstanding bravery whilst pressing on to bomb his target, having been twice wounded, with one of his crew dead and another fatally wounded, and his aircraft crippled and defenceless. At the time No. 61 Sqn was based at Syerston in Nottinghamshire, but this act of bravery occurred just a few days before the squadron moved to Skellingthorpe, where it joined No. 50 Sqn. So began a respect and rivalry between the two squadrons as, with the exception of a short period of two months during early 1944 when No. 61 Sqn moved briefly to Coningsby, the two squadrons operated side by side from Skellingthorpe for the rest of the war.

Having settled in at Skellingthorpe, Les and his crew flew their first training sortie on 4 November, the day after the Düsseldorf raid. The Lancaster Mk III was JA961, which had been built at Chadderton and delivered to the squadron just a few weeks earlier; unfortunately, like many Lancasters at that time, it would not last long and would crash at Melbourne, near York, just three weeks later. The sortie lasted just over four and a half hours and was a good introduction for the crew operating out of its new home. The crew flew two more training sorties on the following day; the first a firing exercise over the sea and the second another cross-country navigation exercise.

Friday 5 November

Took off at 1100 hrs to test our guns over the North Sea and after half an hour we came back at low-level. It was damned good fun. The Land Girls always waved to us. The farmers were not so happy.

Whilst these training sorties provided good opportunities to become familiar with new surroundings, Les just wanted to get on with operations but for the time being at least, he had to remain patient.

Saturday 6 to Tuesday 9 November

Cheesed off! To begin with, Frank (Navigator) was sick, so as a crew we were operationally unfit – that's a good start. Also a raid has been hanging in the balance each day and scrubbed each night, The boys are a bit twitchy, being briefed in the afternoon then getting dressed in flying kit and going out to the kites just as 'two whites' go up from the control tower, signifying operations cancelled. Apparently that's a thing we'll have to get used to.

Wednesday 10 November

Frank is back and once again we are operationally fit, but our luck is out, there are 'ops' tonight but we aren't on, what a bind! However there is a shortage of gunners so Jock, our mid-upper gunner, is going with P/O Litherland and Fred, our rear gunner, in 'B-Baker' with F/Lt. Boulton. 'Good shooting! You lucky people!'. 'Met' (weather forecast) is a dead cert. tonight – the boys know it and are getting ready eagerly as I am writing. You should see their brightly coloured scarves, socks and football jerseys, and their funny looking mascots, such as dolls, which have places of honour in gun turrets and cockpits. That's all for now, I'll get the latest 'gen' from them tomorrow when they get back.

Pilot Officer Litherland was later killed, having been shot down over Berlin during a raid on the night of 15/16 February 1944; he and his bomb aimer are buried in the Berlin 1939–45 War Cemetery and the rest of the crew are commemorated on the Runnymede Memorial near Windsor, which commemorates those aircrew who have no known grave.

Thursday 11 November

The boys did a 'bang-on' job last night. The target was Modane, an important rail tunnel running through the Alps between France and Italy and proved to be a bomb aimer's paradise. Having no searchlights and only four light flak guns, out of the whole squadron only one aircraft was attacked by a fighter, an FW190, but emerged with no damage.

The raid had been against the railway yards on the main line to Italy and caused serious damage to the railway network; no aircraft were lost.

Tuesday 16 November

The afternoon proved to be very boring, the whole squadron was put in the air to test a new system of quick landing. We just 'stooged' about and at 1430 hrs we received a recall by W/T to come in and land on the new system. Everything went off OK and they landed thirteen Lancasters in eighteen minutes – not bad! However, that was not sufficient, and we had to repeat the effort after dark. That was a very 'shaky do'. Actually getting into the main stream around the circuit was the most dangerous. We had two very near misses; one was so close to our tail that Fred (R/G) said he could have reached out of his turret and poked the pilot in the eye. What a line!!

The first three weeks on the squadron had proved frustrating for Les: training sortie after training sortie, whilst the rest of the squadron took part in operations. By the end of their first three weeks they had flown ten daylight training sorties, mainly cross-country and practice bombing exercises, totalling twenty hours of flying. Although it felt frustrating to the crew, the extra hours gave valuable experience in the Lancaster as well as of flying in different airframes as each had its own special characteristics. As an indication of the high losses in airframes it is interesting to note that all six Lancasters flown by the crew prior to their first operational sortie did not survive the winter. Apart from the crash of JA961, the other five were all shot down, three of them during raids on Berlin.

On 17 November, the long wait for operations was over, or so Les believed.

Wednesday 17 November

Tonight's the night (we thought it was anyway). At 1000 hrs gen came through from Group to prepare for 'ops' tonight and F/O Beetham's crew are on. You can imagine how excited we felt as we put on our flying kit and were driven out to the kite to do our NFT, a short daylight air test which every aircraft has before going on 'ops'. Everything was in order except the escape hatches

– the mid-upper hatch blew off as we took-off and the escape hatch in the floor of the bombing compartment wouldn't properly close, so we had them fixed when we landed. 0200 hrs – what a disappointment! Ops scrubbed again because of bad visibility so we had to trail out to the kite and bring back our parachutes, harnesses, helmets, gear etc.

Thursday 18 November

Ops again tonight but not for us, only for 'gen crews' – must be a difficult trip, all we could do was an NFT in 'F-Freddie' for the crew that were flying her tonight. At 1800 hrs I went to watch take-off. It was on the short runway and rather a 'shaky do'. Every kite had to use the whole of the runway and some even went over the boundary before becoming airborne. Out of the nineteen aircraft which took off, two 'boomeranged' [*returned to base with various faults*]; the inter-com of one was U/S [*unserviceable*] and in another the bomb aimer 'passed out'. All aircraft got back safely and only one was slightly 'shot up'. By the way the target was the 'big city' – BERLIN!

The raid on the night of 18/19 November was the start of what was to become known as the Battle of Berlin. A force of 440 Lancasters and four Mosquitoes took part. The target was completely covered by cloud and bombing was scattered.

The following night Les and crew were once again on the battle orders, but once again the operation was scrubbed due to weather. The crew did, however, have an eventful night.

Friday 19 November

Our crew was called by tannoy to the flight offices where we were briefed to do a search over the North Sea for the crew of a Lancaster which had 'ditched' on return from an attack on Ludwigshafen. Met forecast was far from ideal, and as the area we were to search was up and down the Dutch/German coastline, we were warned to be on the alert for German fighters. As it turned out we were fully occupied trying to cope with the atrocious conditions we found on arrival in the search area. It was pouring with rain, cloud base about 500ft and a very nasty sea, which made it difficult to see anything at all except huge waves. Nevertheless we carried on although even turning a Lancaster at that height above the sea was dodgy to say the least. However we carried on until dusk hoping to spot the dinghy but eventually we had to give up with fuel getting low and we returned to base. We spent over four hours searching, and every member of the crew was disappointed at not having been successful in finding the dinghy. In the back of our minds we were all thinking, 'Poor sods, what a way to go. But for the grace of God it might have been us.' A sobering thought.

The following day the crew were told that the conditions under which they had carried out the search were so bad that they were being credited with the first of their tour of thirty operations. So that was it, their first official operational sortie, although it had not been at all what they had imagined! In his diary Les effectively dismisses this as his first operational sortie, as it had not been a major Bomber Command effort.

If he was disappointed by the fact that his first official operational sortie had not been against a major German target, then his disappointment was not to last for long. Just when it was beginning to feel as though it would never happen, the crew were detailed for operations again, but this time it would happen just as Les had always imagined.

Monday 22 November

I walked up to the 'drome at 1000 hrs and immediately knew there were 'ops' cooking. Men were dashing in and out of flight offices; crews in flying kit were piling into transports, and everyone was generally busy. First I saw Mike our pilot, 'Yes, we are on', so I get the crew together and off we go to do our NFT on 'D-Dog' – she's the kite we're taking tonight. One or two minor defects were evident – the escape hatch in the floor of the bombing compartment wasn't quite as free as I like it to be, also the starboard outer temperature gauge was U/S, but that was Don's, the Flight Engineer's problem. At 1300 hrs we landed and handed the kite over to the ground crew for bombing up, refuelling and a final polish.

Main briefing started at 1330 hrs and what do you think? It's the 'Big City' – BERLIN; bags of flap – it's a helluva long trip, at least 1,400 miles there and back, by the route we are taking. I drew my maps and stuck down the route, then got my bombing 'gen', i.e. the bomb-load I was taking; route markers to be seen; technique to be used and which flares to be bombed should the target be obscured by cloud. That over, we all met in the main briefing room where each crew has a good chat about the trip. Needless to say we were all very excited because, to an experienced crew, Berlin is quite an assignment – you can imagine what we felt like to be doing it for our first trip.

Then at 1445 hrs our 'ops' meal was eaten with much relish as though it was our last. As it happened so it was for one crew – but that will come later. Now the great bind of getting dressed. This is what I wore: my ordinary battle dress; two pairs of long silk/wool underpants; white polo sweater; heated electric waistcoat and electric slippers; kapok flying suit; Mae West; parachute harness and helmet. I also carried in my leather 'gen bag' two spare pairs of gloves; torch; goggles; six maps; handker-chiefs and escape kit. You can imagine what a bind it is moving about getting into the aircraft in that outfit. To get from the door of the Lancaster to the bombing compartment was even worse, getting hooked up on one thing and another, climbing over the main spar getting all steamed up. Next, as the bomb aimer I had to check my equipment, the bomb load and settings of the pre-selection switches, look over the camera circuit, check the lens heater, magazine muff and, last but not least, the photoflash. That, I think, is the deadliest thing in the kite. They develop over one million candle power and have been known to blow an aircraft to pieces.

Everything's OK. Mike, our pilot, starts up the four Merlins and each member of the crew checked his equipment – our mid-upper gunner Jock and our rear gunner Fred checked the rotation of gun turrets, operation of guns, ammunition feed. Reg, our wireless operator, checked his various transmitters, receivers and other devices. Frank, our navigator, checked his set, known as 'Gee', and other items of equipment (which are still on the secret list). Finally Don, our engineer, glances at his hundred and one dials to ensure that the four Merlins are fit and healthy, while Mike tries all his controls.

Then the great moment as Mike signals 'chocks away'. Out rush our ground crew to heave at the great wooden blocks which are in front of our wheels. 'OK brakes off', and we taxi round the perimeter track to the take-off point on the runway. It is still daylight and a great sight to see. Lining the runway is a motley collection of ground staff, aircrew not on 'ops', the station CO, the Wing Commander with visitors and friends and, last but not least, the usual crowd of WAAFs, waving goodbye to their boyfriends. At the crucial moment we get an 'Aldis' 'GREEN' [*wireless silence*] from control and with the mighty roar of four Merlins in our ears we give the crowd a quick wave and tear down the runway, Frank reading our airspeed to Mike until we are airborne and 'wheels up'.

Although it is still daylight, dusk is rapidly falling and almost as soon as we set course we find we are in cloud.

For me there is not much to do so I plug in my electric suit, make myself comfortable – if that's possible – and let my thoughts wander. Of course that's fatal, I realize what we are out to do and how frightened I really am; after all, this is my first operational trip. In spite of the unsuitable surroundings I say a prayer to ask for forgiveness for killing so many human beings with the dropping of my bombs. Also prayers to ask for courage, which I seem to lack at the moment, and for a safe flight to enable us to return to the land which I realize I love so much, to relatives and friends, and to my wife who means more to me than anything in the world. To my mind she is braver than I am. She believes I'm in danger seven nights a week yet in reality it is perhaps three, perhaps only one.

At 9,000ft and still climbing we break cloud – it is almost dark yet all around we can see shapes, vague yet resolute, all moving in the same direction. It is rather comforting to know you are not alone in your effort, and from figures given us at briefing we know that for every kite we can see there must be a hundred we can't. Up and up we go – again in cloud, and finally at 20,000ft we level out and settle down to a steady cruising speed. Already we can see the futile attempts of the enemy to stem the attack, all along the Dutch coast the bright flashes of the German 'heavy stuff' light up the clouds. Their prediction is bad though and the shells burst way below us.

Now I get busy – setting up my bombing panel, 'bombs selected', fusing switches 'On', distributor set – and I start my regular bit of 'jamming' to the German radio direction apparatus code-named 'Window'. They love it! From now on things begin to liven up. Far away on the port beam the defences of Bremen are in action against some poor sod off-track. Then Hanover, they shoot up all they can but to no avail, our route, which we rigidly adhered to thanks to the skill of Frank, our navigator, takes us just out of range of their flak. Searchlights try to pick us up, but that's useless, they can't get through the cloud.

On and on we roar passing an occasional track marker put down by PFF. They quickly improve on that and follow up with 'REDS' cascading into 'GREENS' gradually descending into the clouds. These are the ones we bomb. Already I can see the first wave unloading their bombs. At the same time a line of fighter flares goes down, brilliant and bright, parallel to our track about 2 miles away, but don't panic, it's a decoy laid down by our Mosquito boys. Things are getting larger and clearer as we approach the target. Then the final turn in – this is it! I crane my neck in an excited attempt to see everything at once. It is my job to decide in my own mind which of all the target indicators is most accurate. This done I give the necessary correction to Mike our pilot, to get the TIs lined up in my bombsight. At last – 'bomb doors open', but look! Way down below us I see a Halifax, shouldn't like to prang him with my bombs, so we do a quick weave ending up on a parallel course, and with a final, 'left, left, steady' to Mike, I press the 'tit' and up lurches the kite as 4,000lb of death shoot down and, can by can, our incendiaries scatter. Quickly I throw the jettison bars across to ensure that we have no 'hang ups' in the bomb bay, then we straighten up while the camera operates to photograph our aiming point. 'OK camera operated, bomb doors closed,' I shout.

Now I have time to survey the scene. Below us is the capital of the Third Reich at our mercy. The clouds themselves are too thin to hide the destruction which is taking place. Everywhere below us for miles around is burning, throwing up pink and scarlet through the clouds, making it so bright that I could have read a newspaper in my bombing compartment. The vivid yellow explosions of 'cookies' bursting [4,000lb bombs] are so numerous that the figure of forty a minute must be a gross understatement. When we bombed in the fifth wave, they seemed to be bursting all over the target simultaneously. As far as flak is concerned it was very moderate and all fell short bursting about 3,000ft below us.

Across on the port bow I saw a 'plane out of control, falling down to earth with smoke pouring from it, but no fire as far as I could see, so the crew have a fair chance to bale out. Another disconcerting sight was a 'scarecrow' fired by the German 'ack-ack' which burst about 1,000 yards starboard of us. They are supposed to represent a kite on fire, and believe me I was fooled, not having seen one before. It seemed to hang there. Numerous minor explosions followed and clouds of black smoke poured out, after which it just dropped to earth in a mass of flames.

By now we are tearing speedily out of the target area, and ahead everything looks black, offering very inviting cover. This is the danger area really, where fighters usually wait. The red 'Very' signals, which they use to attract one another's attention in the air, were all around us, so, to avoid being 'jumped', Mike did a steady weave for about five minutes. Time passes rather slowly now – I suppose it's because we are keen to get back to base having accomplished our task. However, there are 600 miles to go so there is no need to get over-anxious. Cloud is still our greatest advantage. We pass near the defences of many German cities but the searchlights just can't break through the clouds; consequently the flak is very dispersed and spasmodic. Finally we pass the last track marker in enemy territory, and we alter course for the Dutch coast. Things begin to get quieter, but to be on the safe side we do an occasional banking search to ensure that no enemy night fighters are trying to get us from underneath.

Now all is quiet and Frank, our navigator, gives us the

glad news that according to his calculations we are now crossing the Dutch coast. However our presumed safety is rather premature, because 'wuff' and bang under our nose bursts three rounds of heavy stuff – obviously predicted at us. Away we go into violent evasive tactics while I pile on the agony by jamming their radio location with 'Window'. Again all is quiet – this time for good we hope – as we start letting down from the height of 25,000ft, which we managed to attain after getting rid of our bombs.

Half an hour later at 8,000ft we are able to release our oxygen masks and breathe freely once more. That is a relief that can be appreciated only after wearing one for seven hours. Now the fun starts. Don, our engineer, gets busy passing round to the rest of the crew flasks of hot coffee which refresh us no end, even to the extent of chatting a little on the intercom. Now we can see other kites as they switch on their navigation lights. As the English coast is reached we are in the centre of a great armada, there are hundreds and hundreds of little red, green and white navigation lights – actually of course the kites have been there all the time but without lights we couldn't see them.

Now there is the problem of finding base. We are well below cloud now and can see kites weaving off in all directions, to their various 'dromes – luckily we haven't far to go. We are in our own circuit in no time, passing the usual message, 'Hello Black Swan. This Is Pilgrim "D-Dog". May I pancake please – over?' [*'Pilgrim' is the No. 50 Sqn call-sign when airborne*]. This is acknowledged by the friendly voice of the WAAF R/T operator and we heave a sigh of relief as our wheels finally touch down on the runway.

Back safely, what a great feeling it was to hear the familiar voices of Jock, Fred, Mac and Allan, our ground crew, as they opened the door for us and placed the ladder in position helping us out with all our gear. 'No damage,' we are delighted to tell them. Next stop is the locker rooms where all our flying kit is left behind. We don our greatcoats and caps once more, making our way to intelligence for debriefing. Here we give them all the 'gen': flak, searchlights, icing troubles, fighter opposition, air battles, kites shot down, parachutes and anything else we can think of. After that the inevitable question. 'Are all the boys back?' 'No-one is missing, but there is still time.' Well, that's that! We have supper (or is it breakfast, because it is now 0500 hrs?). The eggs and bacon go down well and we shoot a horrid line until we are too tired to sit up any longer. Then we just quietly slip off to the billets and into bed. I should add that my last thoughts before complete oblivion were concerned with a prayer of thanks for my safe return. So ends our first operation, our baptism of fire.

The total effort against Berlin on the night of 22/23 November was 764 aircraft, which was the largest number of bombers sent against the capital to date. The force consisted of 469 Lancasters, 234 Halifaxes, fifty Stirlings and eleven Mosquitoes. Fortunately for Les on his first major operation, bad weather at the *Luftwaffe*'s night-fighter bases had prevented most from getting airborne, which explains why he had not seen a night fighter all night. Due to the cloud over the target area it was almost impossible to determine the success of the raid but bombing had been spread across a large area of the city and there had been considerable damage to the residential areas. There was also considerable damage to a number of industrial areas. Casualties on the ground were estimated to have been in the order of 2,000. The losses to Bomber Command were relatively small, due to the lack of night fighters, although twenty-six bombers failed to return. One of the eleven Lancasters lost belonged to No. 50 Sqn Warrant Officer J.H. Saxton and his crew are buried in the Berlin 1939–45 War Cemetery.

For the record, the Lancaster flown by Les and his crew

on his first trip to Berlin was JA899 'VN-D', a Mk III built at Chadderton. Like so many others, this airframe would not last the war as it was shot down soon after D-Day during June 1944. Not surprisingly, at seven hours and fifteen minutes, the trip to Berlin was Les's longest sortie to date. His tour of operations was well and truly under way.

CHAPTER SIX

To Berlin and Back, Again and Again and Again . . .

There was no time for the new crew to rest or celebrate their first 'proper' operational sortie and their first trip to the big city; it would certainly not be their last! Having got some well-earned sleep, they were up and about the following morning.

Tuesday 23 November

Up at 1000 hrs and had a bath – and what do you think? Rumours are already circulating about 'ops' tonight. I can't stand the suspense, so instead of waiting until after lunch I go up to the flights and get the 'gen'. Yes, we are on again, and it's Berlin again. Once more we go through exactly the same routine and bomb the heart out of the place. We are not quite so lucky this time; on the way back our flaps became U/S and although the kite is perfectly OK, we would have difficulty landing without flaps, which act as brakes. On getting back to base Mike calls them up and puts the situation to them – 'No, nothing doing.' They don't want a 'prang' in the middle of their 'drome while two squadrons are landing, so they send us to RAF Wittering. There they specialize in flap-less landings at high speeds, having a 3 mile stretch of grass airfield on which to touch down. The landing was exceptionally well executed by Mike – naturally! He did an approach at 130mph and landed safely – to the amazement of the nine WAAFs in flying control who, together with two 'blood wagons' [*ambulances*], had come to watch us 'prang'! RAF Wittering, which, incidentally, is not a bomber station, treated us like heroes. The one word 'Berlin' was like magic to them. We had a smashing supper, followed by a bottle of whisky and cig's – all on the mess. 'Course we had to shoot a line about the trip – they expected it and were genuinely interested. That being well done we went to bed!

'Bomber' Harris decided that his force should return to Berlin again, although this time it would be half the number of the previous night; a total of 383 aircraft took part in the raid on the night of 23/24 November. With the exception of the Halifax and Mosquito Pathfinders, the main bombing force was all-Lancaster. The route chosen was the same as the previous night but this time the weather at the *Luftwaffe*'s night-fighter bases was more favourable and more were able to hassle the main stream; twenty Lancasters failed to return (more than 5 per cent of the Lancaster force despatched). Conditions over Berlin were again cloudy, which meant that the Pathfinders had to use sky-marking techniques, but crews could occasionally see fires still burning from the previous night. The result of the raid was further destruction to residential and industrial areas and casualties on the ground were in the order of 1,500.

Les and his crew had, once again, flown in JA899 'VN-D' on this raid and, at seven hours and forty-five minutes, it was another record airborne time for the crew. Having spent the night at Wittering, they flew JA899 back to Skellingthorpe the following day. The total effort in the past two nights against Berlin had been more than 1,100 bomber sorties and so there were no operations for the Lancaster crews of No. 5 Group the following night; this provided a much needed rest for the crews of No. 50 Sqn.

Wednesday 24 November

At RAF Wittering we got up at 1000 hrs, had breakfast and went to see how the 'erks' were getting on. Unfortunately there were many minor defects, such as missing exhaust manifolds etc. However, by 1500 hrs it was OK so we took off and landed back at base 1530 hrs. Boy-oh-boy! – squadron 'stand down', so we all got changed and went into town for the evening.

Thursday 25 November

The 'powers that be' say the 'Big City' must be bombed again – so here we go, but take-off is put back from 1700 hrs to 2200 hrs – that's bad. At 2130 hrs we were walking out to the kites when 'SCRUBBED' passed round like wildfire – back to bed early.

The rest was soon over, however, as Bomber Command returned to Berlin on the night of 26/27 November. Once again, Les was on operations. It was to be his third raid on Berlin in five nights. On this occasion Bomber Command detailed an all-Lancaster main force of 450 aircraft to attack Berlin and a smaller force of 157 Halifaxes and twenty-one Lancasters was detailed to attack Stuttgart as a diversionary raid.

Friday 26 November

Before recounting the events of today I should like to point out that my first two raids on Berlin were a 'piece of cake'. Everything was in our favour – there was cloud at varying heights over the continent, yet Britain was comparatively cloud-free. The operation tonight showed how different things could be.

Take-off was as usual for Berlin, about 1630 hrs. The

route was different, however, we climbed and climbed going straight out and we were well over France when operational height was reached. The first few hundred miles were unusually quiet, no night fighters came to meet us, and cloud cover was fairly regular. But these conditions were short-lived. Suddenly, as we came within range of Frankfurt, the cloud disappeared like magic and the sight, which to me was new, was rather alarming. Dead ahead and on our starboard beam were masses of searchlights. Already many kites had been 'coned' and were being shot at in no mean fashion, and to make matters worse, enemy night fighters were putting down two lines of flares bang across our track, so we just had to go straight in, neck or nothing so to speak. Still, we made it OK, but I saw two Lancs go down in flames. Needless to say we went flat-out over that area and we were jolly glad to be able to turn on to the last leg to Berlin. Things went very quiet again for a while, but this good visibility had us wondering, I'll never trust Met again. They said there would be low cloud over the target to give us good cover, but was there hell?

The first signs of Berlin were the searchlight belts of the outer defences. As we approached two kites were coned, one on either side of us, so we had a more or less un-molested passage through the inner belt. Those two kites took terrific punishment from the flak, which was 'spot on', yet they were both weaving frantically to escape when we lost sight of them. We were now close enough to the target to see the effect of our predecessors in the first wave and it really was terrific. The whole of the target area was a sea of flames, with two particular spots rather like volcanoes. Even from 4 miles high the glare was so intense you could clearly see streets and build-ings amid the inferno. I opened our bomb doors and down went the whole load on a cluster of ground markers in the centre of Berlin. While all this was taking place our W/Op, Reg, reported two combats, and I was just in time to see the second, a Lancaster, going down in flames. As it began to spin, four parachutes very smartly appeared. I'm afraid the rest of the crew went down with the kite.

Having dropped our bombs, the old kite – VN-F – gained a new lease of life, and we started climbing rapidly into the dark sky ahead of us. However, after a few minutes the rear gunner reported condensation trails forming behind us, so we reluctantly had to descend a few thousand feet. You don't want to give away your position if you can avoid it. Nothing more of interest happened until we drew near to Hamburg. There we found stretching in the direction of Hanover, a great wall of searchlights about 50 miles long. The usual flak batteries were there too, working in co-operation with the searchlights, as the Germans do so well. There was no going round this lot, so it was nose down, maximum revs, and headlong into it. Yet they got us straight away. Mike did a terrific dive to port, followed by a steep climbing turn to starboard. Simultaneously the flak opened up, and then without a word of warning our intercom went as dead as a doornail. There was a horrible silence, which has to be experienced to be appreciated, but the comforting thought was that the kite was still going through the usual evasive tactics. Apparently the kite was not damaged and Mike was still master of the situation.

When things quietened down he got the emergency intercom working, whereupon our W/Op, Reg, informed us that in the first furious dive our HT batteries broke loose and sailed down the fuselage, and now he was about to retrieve them. Having done that, everything was under control again. As far as the enemy was concerned they gave us a few more rounds of heavy stuff at the Dutch coast and that was that. Fighters – nil. Little did we know it but here our troubles really began. First of all we ran into dense cloud. Then a message came through from base diverting us to RAF Pocklington, near York, because Skellingthorpe was fog-bound. After a spot of quick thinking by Frank, our navigator, we altered course for our new destination. Then the old kite starts icing up and we start losing height hand over fist. Luckily freezing height was 5,000ft and we found that nearer the deck we thawed out and at 1,000ft we crossed the coast near the Humber. From there Frank directed us on radar straight to RAF Pocklington. Vis was bad but we could see the flare path, and Mike called them up in double quick time. This was where we got our first shock. They wouldn't take us; said visibility was not good enough and they too diverted us to the next 'drome, RAF Melbourne.

Things were really serious now. Obviously the weather was deteriorating rapidly, and we were running short of fuel, so off we went – no messing about! We got into Melbourne circuit and called them up. There was much more fog here than at the previous 'drome, but we just HAD to get down here so in we went. The glow of the flarepath was just visible through the fog and by a miraculous combination of good piloting by Mike and good luck, we lined up on the runway first shot to touch down on our first attempt.

There's no doubt about it; this was our lucky night. We were the first of the squadron to land here, and judging by the messages passing on RT things were really chaotic. We had already heard two of the squadron ordered to head out to sea and bale out because their fuel was down to nil, so we parked the kite as instructed by air traffic control and piled out, getting as far from the runway as possible and only just in time. Immediately behind us 'A-Able' [JB485 – P/O Toovey] came in and swerved off the runway, becoming bogged down in the soft ground, then down came 'X-Xray' [DV377 – P/O Weatherstone] who missed the runway completely, hit a van then slap into 'A-Able'. Both kites caught fire.

However, the crews were prepared for anything at this stage and were all out in a flash and no one was even injured. The usual RAF Standard 8 van was on airfield duty. Sadly the driver of the van was killed. Actually a wheel had passed over the vehicle and the van's engine was partly buried in the ground. While all this had been taking place, 'K-King' [*ED393 – F/Sgt J.W. Thompson*] had been trying to land and, after many unsuccessful attempts, hit a farmhouse. The only survivor was the rear gunner. The poor farmer and his wife were also killed. We subsequently heard that the crash was due to running out of fuel. Whether or not this is true we shall never know. No. 50 Sqn lost three Lancasters in the UK 'A-Able'; 'X-Xray' and 'K-King', and 'N-Nan' [*DV178 – P/O J. C. Adams*] was missing over Germany.

So the whole operation cost us four Lancasters, although thankfully only two crews. After such an experience, we were all well and truly fagged out, and when quarters were found for us we literally flaked out, some even before they got into bed.

Bomber Command's effort on the night of 26/7 November succeeded in causing some confusion amongst the German defences. Both the Berlin and Stuttgart forces had transited outbound across northern France together before they split. The German defences were led to believe that Stuttgart was the main target and it was in that area that the majority of Bomber Command's losses occurred. The main force attacking Berlin arrived in the target area to find the weather generally clear, and there was considerable damage to industrial and residential areas. Unfortunately the main force had become scattered and more Lancasters were shot down on the return leg. Of the 443 detailed to attack Berlin, twenty-eight were shot down over enemy territory and fourteen more crashed back in England. This represents an overall loss rate for the Lancaster force that night of nearly 10 per cent.

Of the thirteen Lancasters from No. 50 Sqn that had taken

off from Skellingthorpe early that evening, one returned early with engine trouble and one was lost over Germany. Five of the remaining aircraft crashed on landing back in the UK and only six returned to Skellingthorpe.

Les's diary refers to Lancaster ED393 VN-K that crashed into a farmhouse whilst attempting to land at Pocklington. It came down at Canal Head, Hayton, 2 miles to the south-east of the village of Pocklington. Five of the crew were killed, including the captain, Flight Sergeant Thompson. In addition to the rear gunner, Sergeant T. A. Wyllie, whom Les refers to in his diary as having survived, one of the other gunners, Sergeant C. R. Corbett, also had a lucky escape and survived. The two occupants of the farmhouse were Mrs Gertrude Bird, aged 69, and Mr Percy Palucy, aged 41.

The fog covering much of the east of England was still there the following day, and prevented the crew from returning to Skellingthorpe. The crew were stuck at Melbourne for the day with no change of clothing and no money.

Saturday 27 November

At RAF Melbourne, we got up at about 1100 hrs, had breakfast and then went out to survey the damage. 'A-Able' and 'X-Xray' were completely written off. We hadn't a hole in our kite at all, but I found a hundred 4lb incendiary bombs jammed up in the bomb bay, so I got the armourers out to remove them. We found that we were stuck there in dense fog with absolutely nothing but the flying suits which we were wearing from the operation the night before, not even any money!

Nothing daunted us and we managed to get the MT section at RAF Melbourne to provide us with transport to take us into York. With the odd pound we had managed to borrow we were dropped off in the centre and there we saw a pub called the King's Arms. It was situated on the side of the River Ouse, down the steps from the main street overlooked by one of the main bridges in York. There was a wide area of quayside outside the pub and there we established ourselves. We quickly realized that it was a popular pub with the army boys but as soon as we explained our appearance and the fact that we were bombing Berlin the previous night, all barriers disappeared and they were falling over themselves to buy beer for us.

Nearly sixty years later, Les returned to York and he found the Kings Arms where he and his crew had spent the evening back in November 1943. Nothing seemed to have changed and it was very much the old pub that he had remembered. It was, indeed, a very nostalgic moment and memories came flooding back.

The crew were stuck at Melbourne for a second day but eventually, late in the afternoon, there was enough of a weather clearance to return to Skellingthorpe. Once back at base, they were able to enjoy a few days of rest.

Sunday 28 November

Weather was still duff but at 1600 hrs the fog cleared enough for us to take off and return to base.

Monday 29 November

Squadron 'stand down'. It was good to get dressed and see Lincoln again.

Tuesday 30 November

'Ops' tonight but just as we were going out to the kite it was scrubbed. Loud cheers; the blokes just dumped their kit and dashed off to town.

Thursday 2 December

NFTs this morning, sure to be 'ops' tonight, weather is 'bang on'. Briefing was at 1330 hrs but when we got there we found that we had been taken off the operation. There was an American war correspondent who wanted to go on a Berlin operation. Although he had wanted to use our kite, the flight commander, Flt Lt Boulton, thought that he, having a 'gen crew', ought to take the American. Ironically, they didn't come back. I knew the bomb aimer very well; he was one of the best-liked chaps on the squadron. They had done twenty-eight trips, and this was to have been their last. Sadly it was!

The target for Bomber Command on the night of 2/3 December was once again Berlin, the fifth raid against the capital in just two weeks. Not counting the first, on the night of 18/19 November, before Les and his crew had flown their first operational sortie, this was the first night that Les stayed behind from a raid against the 'big city' and had to wait nervously back at Skellingthorpe. Bomber Command's effort that night was essentially an all-Lancaster force of more than 450 aircraft, with no other diversionary raids and only a couple of minor operations taking place. The raid was successful in that there was considerable damage to industrial areas across the city. Unfortunately, however, bomber losses were high. Errors in the wind forecast had caused the main stream to become scattered and forty aircraft were lost, mainly due to the heavy night fighter activity.

The No. 50 Sqn Lancaster lost during the raid, and the one referred to in Les's diary, was DV325 captained by Flight Lieutenant Boulton, which was shot down over the target area. Unknown to Les at the time of his diary entry, Boulton and four of his crew members, including Les's good friend Flight Sergeant Forrester, managed to bale out and were taken as prisoners of war. The American war correspondent, Mr L.L. Bennett, was also fortunate to escape with his life. Sadly, however, two of the crew were killed: the navigator, Pilot Officer A.M. Watson, and the mid-upper gunner, Sergeant R.F. Moody.

The fifth raid against Berlin marked the end of what was

later to be considered the opening phase of the battle and Harris decided to give his crews a break from the 'big city'. By now, Les and his crew had been on operations just two weeks. If they had not before realized the horror of war, then they certainly did now; fifteen of their squadron colleagues had been killed during the two weeks, all on operations against Berlin, and several more were either wounded or had been taken as prisoner of war.

Les had now settled in to life on a Bomber Command operational squadron. His diary records what a typical day on a Lancaster bomber station was like.

The first indication of anything taking place was a tannoy announcement, sometimes as early as 1000 hrs if it was a late afternoon take-off (on many occasions, 1000 hrs was early for us. We may have only been in bed for three or four hours if the previous night's operation had been a late take-off). We sometimes operated on two consecutive nights and on the 22nd, 23rd and 26th November, 1943 we did three Berlin operations within five nights. The first tannoy call was usually, 'Crews report to their sections at "such and such" hours', so off to the bombing section I would go. The target was not revealed at that stage, but details of bomb loads, high explosive and incendiary, were given – usually one 4000lb high explosive bomb plus a number of 1000lb and 500lb bombs and cans of 4lb incendiaries. The load depended on the distance to the target of course. The sequence of dropping was explained in order to maintain stability of the aircraft, but the armourers set this up for us when bombing-up the aircraft. We were also informed of any 'extras' we were to distribute over Germany *en route* to the target, like news leaflets in German and forged ration coupons for meat, butter and cheese.

On most operations we were detailed to handle the 'Window – bundles of narrow metallic strips which we pushed out at intervals in order to blot out the radar screens of the enemy defences and, to a certain extent, the night fighters' radar. To end our briefing the Bombing Leader usually said, 'Get a good straight bombing run, YOU are in charge, identify the correct target indicators, don't be fooled by German dummy fires, and, bring back an aiming point photograph.' This was achieved by an aerial camera fitted in the floor of the bombing compartment and wired into the bombing circuit, together with a one million candle-power photo-flash which was released with the bombs. With the aid of a built-in delay it was timed to explode as my bombs hit the target, and hopefully showing the aiming point.

The usual pattern was to get the main force of 700 to 800 bombers over the target in about twenty-five minutes, split into separate waves of five minutes with the most experienced crews in the first wave and the 'sprogs' like us in the last wave. It was no picnic being in the last wave, the night fighters had more time to find you, and if you were damaged either by flak or by being attacked by Ju88s, you fell behind the last wave and you were a 'sitting duck'. The secret was, regardless of circumstances, to be alert at all times difficult as it might be having already been airborne for many hours.

Next was the NFT [night flying test]. This was a flight lasting about half an hour during which every member of the crew checked his equipment. My task was to check the intercom, then the bomb sight, sighting head, and bombing computer, all the electrics in the bombing compartment, the front turret for rotation and elevation and that the gun sight was working OK. Lastly, I had to check that the escape hatch, which was in the floor of the bombing compartment, opened correctly and was safely locked too, because the bomb aimer would lie full length on it when over enemy territory.

Occasionally the routine would be changed, the NFT would come first, followed by section briefing depending on the time of take-off, which could be brought forward or put back taking into account the Met forecast both at base and over the target. As most winter operations were to more distant targets, Berlin, Leipzig, Frankfurt, Nuremberg, Stuttgart, Brunswick, Munich etc., all of which incurred eight-hour trips, the routine was either to take off about 1600 hrs in the last of the daylight and land on return about midnight, or to have a late take-off and return at about daybreak the next morning.

Finally, there was the main briefing attended by all pilots and their crews. The target details would come first from the squadron commander, together with the route to be taken, both out and back, as displayed on the huge briefing room map. Attention was drawn to the proximity of heavily defended areas to be avoided, and details of enemy defences to be penetrated in order to reach the target. Information on enemy night fighter activities which were to be expected on our route, both out and back, were given by the Intelligence Officer, together with advice on what to do in the event of being shot down.

The Met Officer came next with a forecast of the weather we could expect during take-off, while climbing through cloud to our operational height of 21,000ft, over the target, and finally what to expect on return to base. Sometimes we would take off knowing that the weather on return to base would be 'duff', in which case we would be given various alternative possible landing areas. If necessary, updated information would be sent by radio directing us to specific bases free from fog, usually further north in Yorkshire.

When main briefing was over the odd two or three hours left would be spent relaxing – if that was possible – and having the traditional 'ops' meal of bacon and eggs. Yes, real eggs! A ritual before take-off on 50 Sqn was to listen in the mess to the record of the Andrew

Sisters singing 'The Shrine of Saint Cecilia'. If you were a superstitious type it was a must, if not then you still listened to it because it was considered extremely unlucky not to have done so, and you did not want to push your luck – not to mention the wrath of your crew if they found out. Final preparations before going out to the aircraft, apart from collecting my parachute and Mae West, were personal. In a leather satchel, which incidentally was my wife's old school bag, I carried my RAF escape kit, my target maps, my silk gloves and leather gauntlets – both RAF issue. It also contained my personal escape kit, which consisted of a razor, shaving cream, tooth brush and paste, soap, comb and sticking plaster, all were held in a fifty Craven A cigarette tin. I reckoned if you were shot down and hoped to evade capture and get back to your squadron it was essential to be able to look respectable.

On arrival at the aircraft I stowed my 'chute, clipped on my one-man dinghy (I couldn't swim!), put my escape kit and evasion tin inside my battledress blouse, and draped my chain of lucky charms around the bomb-sight (for the record – a rabbit's foot, a Cornish pixie, a silver threepenny bit, a Lincoln imp, and a suspender). Finally we all had the ritual 'pee' on the Lancaster tail wheel for luck and then we were off. Believe it or not, as we climbed away from base into the blackness, I said my prayers for forgiveness for the killing of innocent people with my bombs, and for a safe return back to base.

Ever since man first took flight, some aircrew have been notoriously superstitious. For some it is merely a matter of not walking under ladders, but for others there have been a variety of routines before flight or the odd lucky charm or two carried on the person whilst flying. The carrying of lucky charms seems to be particularly evident during wartime operations and this attitude to luck was purely down to the individual; it was a case of whatever worked for one would be laughed at by another but superstition and luck was certainly taken seriously by many of the No. 50 Sqn aircrew at Skellingthorpe. It was considered somewhat dicey if one of the sergeant aircrew had not listened at least once to 'The Shrine of St Cecilia', written by Pern Jokern and Carroll Loveday and recorded by the Andrew Sisters in 1941, on the record player in the mess before taking off on an operation.

Our home is a shambles, all I treasured has gone.
The town seems deserted, everyone's so forlorn.
A storm came from up above but somehow it missed
The shrine of Saint Cecilia.

The bells in the chapel never ring anymore.
The clock in the steeple can't tell time as before.
But up on the hillside, stands a place heaven blest
The shrine of Saint Cecilia.

Each day at eventide
When I seek haven from my daily care
You'll find me by her side.
It seems so peaceful there.

I kneel in my solitude and silently pray
That heaven will protect you, dear, and there'll come a
    day
The storm will be over and that we'll meet again
At the shrine of Saint Cecilia.

Each day at eventide
When I seek haven from my daily care
You'll find me by her side
It seems so peaceful there.

I kneel in my solitude and silently pray
That heaven will protect you, dear, and there'll come a
    day
The storm will be over and that we'll meet again
At the shrine of Saint Cecilia.

At the shrine of Saint Cecilia.

It was not uncommon for one member of the crew to ask if another had listened to the 'Shrine'. If the answer was no then that individual was sent back to the mess to listen to it 'pronto'. On one occasion the record was broken because someone had dropped it and without delay a dispatch rider was sent to Nottingham to purchase a replacement.

A sad routine which seemed to take place every week at Skellingthorpe during this period was the regular visit of the RAF Police to the sergeants' mess. The Nissen huts generally accommodated ten NCOs each with the ablution block about 100 yards away. Everyone had their routine for washing and shaving but most carried their toiletries in either an empty gas mask haversack or a toilet bag given by family or friends. To avoid carrying their toiletries to and from the ablution block, most usually left their bag on the coat pegs along the wall of the toilet block. Consequently, as crews were shot down or missing their toilet kit was left hanging there.

To try and deal with the situation an announcement would often be made on the tannoy system and a notice would go up in the sergeants' mess:

AN INSPECTION OF THE NCOs ABLUTION BLOCK WILL TAKE PLACE AT 1000 HRS

To the aircrew, what the notice really meant was 'Take your toiletries back to your Nissen hut tomorrow morning because the RAF Police will be collecting all the toilet kits of missing aircrew at 1000 hrs.' It was a stark reminder of the reality of life on an operational station.

When not flying on operations, Les and his colleagues took the opportunity to go into Lincoln and have a few drinks with locals and other servicemen. Any time to relax from the stress of operations was most welcome, although RAF aircrew were not admired by all, as Les recorded:

It didn't take long for two of the young bloods in our

crew to 'get organized'. Reg, our W/Op, and Fred, our
R/G, were in Lincoln with a couple of ATS girls having
a drink one night and they happened to choose a pub
that was near to the local drill hall. Frank and I were
invited to join them. There happened to be a battalion
dance in the drill hall and, as arranged, we followed Reg
and Fred later in the evening. Well, it might have been
just to meet the two ATS girls, Ena and Joan, but it
became obvious to us that to the 'squaddies' we were
two more 'Brylcreem boys' which, to them, were two too
many. It was not long before Frank and I, whilst harm-
lessly sipping our first pint of beer, realized that from the
sea of khaki we were receiving many hostile glances. We
were also in a very vulnerable position, up on a balcony
with a narrow spiral staircase between us and the door.
As discreetly as we could we gradually edged to the top
of the staircase but half way down our way was
obstructed by two larger-than-life lance corporals. We
feared the worst but, as it happened, it was just a question of stepping aside to give them the right of way.
Nevertheless we decided not to push our luck any more,
we said our 'good nights' and made for the door while
the path to the exit was clear.

Les and his crew were on operations on the night of 3/4
December but this time for a change the target was not Berlin.
Instead the effort was against the city of Leipzig, which on 9
November 1938 had been the scene of the Nazi destruction of
several Jewish synagogues and establishments on a night that
later became known as *Kristallnacht*. Like Berlin, Leipzig was
deep into the heart of Germany and was a major target for
Bomber Command in its efforts to destroy key installations in
connection with Germany's fighter aircraft and ballbearing
industries.

The night of 3/4 December was to be the first of two visits
to the city by Les and his crew during their tour of operations.
After briefing they were told that their aircraft, DV376 'F-

Freddie' was at Waddington. The crew that had flown it on the previous night's operation to Berlin had landed there on return. Les and his crew were transported there, where they joined the Australians of No. 463 (RAAF) Sqn for the raid. Take-off was not due until late and so the crew had some time to spare. Being a major RAF station, the facilities at Waddington were considerably better than at Skellingthorpe. Les went to the sergeants' mess, which to him seemed more like a hotel when compared to the mess he had been used to, and he spent the next hour or so lounging around in a nice hot bath – a somewhat more relaxing way to prepare for the night ahead than usual.

For the Leipzig raid, the main force of 527 aircraft was a mix of Lancasters and Halifaxes. The route was a familiar one for Les. It involved taking up a heading straight towards Berlin, with little or no deviation due to the distance to the target and the balance between fuel and bomb load critical. A Mosquito diversionary raid towards Berlin had some success in taking some of the night fighters away from the main force as it turned south towards Leipzig.

Friday 3 December

Although half the squadron kites were still at other 'dromes they would have more 'ops' tonight so we were taken by lorry to RAF Waddington complete with flying kit to do the Leipzig operation from there in 'F-Freddie'. It's a pre-war peacetime station. We were briefed with No. 463 Sqn (Aussies) and as take-off was not until 2230 hrs I had a bath in the mess (quite a pleasure in the permanent station's quarters compared with the Nissen huts of 'Skelly'). I kept thinking to myself that if we get shot down tonight I will at least be clean!

Our take-off was OK but it was not so for one of the Lancasters of No. 467 Sqn. It collided on the perimeter track with one of the kites from No. 61 Sqn and took the wing clean off. Jock Grey and his crew (with Taffy Jones, the bomb aimer) were in the No. 61 Sqn kite but got away with it.

All went well until we got within 50 miles of Berlin when during a banking search, Jock (M/UG) spotted an Me110 getting into position underneath us to attack. Off we went weaving like the clappers and lost him before he knew where he was. OK, we turn off for Leipzig and, just as I line up on the target and get the bomb doors open, another Me110 comes tearing across from the starboard quarter to port bow. He sat there waiting to turn in to attack so Mike did a pretty fierce sideslip, or so it felt, and shook him off. 'Twenty degrees port, Skipper – OK – steady – steady – bombs gone – camera operating – OK – bomb doors closed – WEAVE LIKE HELL!'

Away we went and were just congratulating ourselves on 'pranging' the centre of the city when Fred's frantic voice came over the intercom. 'For Christ's sake, corkscrew starboard!' Down we went with not a sound, then Fred again, 'It's up to you, Jock – my guns are frozen up'. 'Keep going – he's following us round.' Round and down we went and this time – crash – a string of red hot cannon shells went flying past my starboard window, so near I could have reached out and touched them. As I sat down there in the nose I thought, 'This is it boys!' and prepared for the inevitable, 'JUMP, JUMP!' However, it didn't come. Jock blazed away and down went a Ju88.

Then we had time to survey the damage. The starboard wing was riddled. No. 2 tank was hit and all the fuel gone, also the flaps were damaged and probably the tyres were burst. It was a toss-up whether we had enough fuel to get us back across the Channel. We jettisoned everything movable, bomb carriers, bomb containers, guns, ammunition etc. and with fingers crossed we made it OK. Flying Control would not give us permission to land at Skellingthorpe in case we had a damaged undercarriage and crashed on the runway, making the base U/S. We were diverted to RAF Wittering where Mike did a spot-on landing on their uneven grass runway. The time was 0815 hrs and we were all in.

By the time the crew had landed at Wittering they had been airborne just under eight hours. It had been quite a night, being briefed at Skellingthorpe, taking off from Waddington and landing at Wittering. The raid had been successful in terms of the bombing results achieved, due to accurate marking by the Pathfinders and because most of the bombers reached the target area. However, a number of bombers were lost on the southerly return leg when they ran into heavy defences. That said, it did prove to be the most successful raid against Leipzig of the war.

Having had just a couple of hours of rest at Wittering, the crew returned to Skellingthorpe in a different Lancaster the following morning.

Saturday 4 December

At 1100 hrs Smithy and his crew brought a Lanc down to RAF Wittering to collect us and flew us back to base, leaving 'F-Freddie' there to get her starboard wing amputated – the main spar was shot away. It was a very dodgy trip. We were lucky to survive. We did, thanks again to Mike, our pilot. On landing our seven day leave passes were waiting for us. To Hell with sleep!

Now due for a few days of well-earned rest, Les had time to reflect on his first two weeks of operations.

We had completed our first four operations, three to Berlin and one to Leipzig, and the net result was 50 Sqn lost seven Lancasters, shot down, crashed or ditched – who knows? Anyway, forty-nine of our aircrew were missing and we had done only four operations! But we had been extremely lucky ourselves. The first Berlin was straightforward but frightening. On the second Berlin we had trouble with our flaps and on returning to base we were not allowed to land. We were diverted to RAF Wittering, which, at the time, was non-operational. There we could do a flapless high speed landing or crash in peace. Wittering was at that time an all-grass airfield. Repairs were effected the next day and we flew back to Skellingthorpe.

On our third Berlin we were diverted to RAF Melbourne. I dealt with that in detail in my operational report. On 3 December 1943 we did our fourth operation, which was to Leipzig. That was horrendous. We were shot up, severely damaged, refused permission to land at Skellingthorpe and ordered to land at RAF Wittering. We were lucky to survive. The next day – 4 December – F/O Smith and his crew brought a Lancaster to Wittering and flew us back to base. I believe our Lanc was a write-off.

We were then due for our operational aircrew seven days' rest leave. We collected our leave passes and headed for the train. I changed trains at Newark, boarded the Kings Cross to Edinburgh express and promptly fell asleep. When home at Billingham my wife remarked that there seemed to be a lot of activity in the air. I went outside to have a look and, sure enough, the sky seemed to be full of Lancasters. Then the truth dawned on me. No. 6 Group of Bomber Command were operating from bases in North Yorkshire, and not many miles away was RAF Middleton St George. And what were they doing, air tests? NFTs of course and why? There were to be operations that night and all aircraft had to be air tested before briefing. Then the air-craft were handed over to the ground staff to refuel and the armourers to bomb up (a tiring and time consuming task, especially if they had 15 x 1,000lb bombs to wind up into the bomb bay. I explained all this to Margaret and she turned and said 'Oh, so now I know when you are operating when I see all these Lancs having their air tests.' I could see that she was not happy. Previously she never knew when I was actually on operations, but now she was going to worry.

I put on my thinking cap. How could I reduce the worry to a minimum? I came up with what I thought was the solution. Immediately we landed after an operation we were always debriefed then went to the mess for breakfast, and in the mess was a public telephone, so that at least she would know that I was back safely. I would send her a fictitious telegram, and to make it more interesting the first letter of the first word would be the same as the first letter of the target, e.g.:

Brenda coming tomorrow	**B**erlin
Frank arrived yesterday	**F**rankfurt
Leave due on Saturday	**L**eipzig

It worked fine, and the icing on the cake was when Margaret switched on the radio for the morning news and heard where Bomber Command had been during the night. In those days the front pages of all newspapers was devoted to details of the night's operations, so she kept the front page of each *Daily Express* which had covered reports of the major operations in which I had taken part.

The system worked well and the result was that Les has many of the original telegrams he sent Margaret during his tour of operations, together with the associated *Daily Express* coverage of the operations, in the scrapbook of memorabilia that he put together after the war.

The seven days of leave were spent just as it should be for any married couple. There was so much to catch up on before the time inevitably came for them to say their goodbyes once more. Les returned to Skellingthorpe the following week. There was much to catch up on back at base, not only from his crew colleagues but from those of the squadron as well. It had, however, been a quiet week for Bomber Command, with only minor operations taking place.

The Leipzig raid on the night of 3/4 December had, in fact, been the Command's last major effort and so Les was relieved that he had not missed out on any of the action. That changed on 16 December when the crews were called for briefing. It was to be Berlin again but not for the Beetham crew. They were, however, required to carry out an NFT on ED856 'VN-A', which lasted just thirty minutes. Following the disappointment of the previous raid against Berlin there had been no raids against the capital for two weeks and this marked the start of a second phase of operations in the Berlin offensive.

The raid on the night of 16/17 December involved an all-Lancaster force of nearly 500 aircraft and was successful in terms of bombing results achieved and the relatively few aircraft lost over enemy territory. However, bad weather back at the various bases doubled the losses to fifty aircraft in total.

As the nights became longer the take-offs were brought forward, which meant that the main bomber force could be over the target during the mid-evening and back on the ground by midnight – quite a luxury as it meant getting more sleep. Harris decided to leave the capital alone for a few nights and so Les's next operation, on the night of 20 December, was near enough an all-out effort against Frankfurt. This was the crew's first (and would be their only) operation to Frankfurt. Compared to their previous raids on Berlin and Leipzig, Frankfurt was to be a much shorter 'hop' at over two hours less flight time.

The aircraft they were allocated was the legendary ED588 'VN-G', more affectionately known to its crews as the lucky 'G-George'. It was one of more than 2,000 Lancaster Mk IIIs built by A.V. Roe & Co at the Newton Heath/Chadderton production plants and was first delivered to No. 97 Sqn at

Coningsby in February 1943. It then moved to No. 50 Sqn at Skellingthorpe in April and flew its first operational sortie with its new squadron against Essen on the night of 30 April. When Mike Beetham got it airborne just before 5.30 p.m. on 20 December, it was the start of the aircraft's fifty-first operational sortie.

The crew landed safely soon after 11.05 p.m. after an uneventful trip. From Bomber Command's perspective, however, the raid had not gone particularly well. The target area was almost totally covered by cloud, which made marking difficult for the Pathfinders. Decoy fires on the ground had also caused some confusion and led to bombing becoming scattered over a large area.

Monday 20 December

Ah! I sense a change. Bags of enthusiasm among the crews! The target is Frankfurt, a change from the long Berlin stooges. The trip was uneventful, and a failure I suspect. PFF 'boobed' I think. The bombs seemed to be all over an area of about 20 miles wide. I guess we shall have to go back there again. For a new crew, prior to Frankfurt we had only done four operations; three on Berlin and one on Leipzig. Frankfurt was at least a change for us but it was a costly night for No. 50 Sqn. We lost two good crews.

The losses referred to were the crews of Wing Commander E. Pullen and Pilot Officer J. L. Heckendorf. Pullen and Heckendorf are both buried in the Durnbach Cemetery, as are six of their colleagues, although the other six members of the two crews managed to bale out and were taken as prisoners of war. The legendary 'G-George' went on to complete at least 125 operational sorties, all but the first ten of which were flown with No. 50 Sqn from Skellingthorpe. To put this amazing statistic into perspective, more than 7,300 Lancasters were built but only thirty-four completed 100 or more operational sorties and maybe only a handful flew more than ED588. Sadly, however, its luck eventually ran out whilst operating with No. 50 Sqn on the night of 29/30 August 1944 when it was one of fifteen Lancasters that failed to return from Königsberg; all but one of Flying Officer Anthony Carver's crew were killed. The highest number of operational sorties flown by a Lancaster is believed to be 140, flown by ED888 'PM-M2' or 'Mike-Squared' as it became known, the majority of which were flown with No. 103 Sqn at Elsham Wolds.

There was time for another major effort against Berlin before Christmas, although Les and his crew were not involved. An all-Lancaster main force of more than 350 aircraft took part in another raid against the capital on the night of 23/24 December. The target was covered by cloud and technical problems with H2S led to variable marking by the Pathfinders, which in turn led to variable bombing accuracy by the main force. This raid also marked the smallest tonnage of bombs dropped against the capital since the offensive began (a total of less than 1,300 tons) and the raid was not considered particularly successful.

There were no operations by Bomber Command over the Christmas period and all across the bomber bases aircrew and ground crew alike were able to relax, for a few days at least.

The next major effort took place on the night of 29/30 December; again the target was Berlin. The Beetham crew were on the operations board at Skellingthorpe and this was to be their fourth visit to the capital in just six operations. On this occasion it was another maximum effort with over 700 bombers taking part, two-thirds of which were Lancasters and the other third Halifaxes. This was the first time that a large force of Halifaxes had been used against Berlin for over a month. The route chosen was a southerly one which, combined with various diversionary raids by Mosquitoes, created confusion amongst the German defence system as to where the main force was heading. When the main force eventually arrived over Berlin the target area was covered by cloud and most of the bombs fell in the southern parts of the city. The confusion created by the route and the diversionary raids proved successful in that bomber losses were relatively light, a total of twenty aircraft, which represented overall losses of less than 3 per cent. The Beetham crew flew LL744 'VN-B' or 'B-Beetham' as they affectionately called it, and the sortie was seven and a half hours long. Les's diary entry immediately after the raid, would suggest that the trip had been uneventful. However, there is a further entry made the following day which indicates otherwise:

Wednesday 29 December

My fourth Berlin. No report in my diary.

Thursday 30 December

Berlin! The usual routine took place. (We were getting used to it now.) A briefing; then an operational meal, then off to the flights to collect our flying gear and parachutes. Take-off was about dusk at 1630 hrs. On return to base it was first debriefing; then our breakfast followed by the coded telegram to Margaret and then to bed. It was probably about 0500 hrs and it seemed that we had hardly time to get to sleep when the door of our Nissen hut flew open and in marched two SPs, shouting, 'Get dressed and report to the flight offices immediate!' No peace for the wicked, so they say. Having reported 'no damage' at debriefing, we were astounded to be asked by the Wing/Co, 'So what's that bloody great hole in your starboard wing?' Transport was waiting outside to take the crew out to dispersal where our Lancaster and the ground crew were waiting for us. Sure enough, standing underneath the aircraft we could see the sky through a gaping hole in the starboard wing.

    To get a better look we climbed aboard and looking down from the cockpit we could see there was the exact outline in red paint of a 30lb incendiary bomb and a hole about 4ft long. Obviously it had been dropped by another aircraft from above us. There was the perfect outline in the horizontal position on the wing where it hit us. The damage was between the fuselage and the starboard inner engine. The bomb had gone right through the inner-wing petrol tank and out through the bottom without exploding. Luckily, we had used most of the petrol in that tank on our way to the target, but Don, our engineer, had remarked that Mike must have been a bit heavy with the boost to get back to base quickly. The fuel gauge for the starboard inner petrol tank read 'NIL'. So Lancaster 'VN B-Beetham' was not fit for 'ops' that night, you don't replace a damaged wing and a petrol tank in five minutes, it was a major job for the ground crew. Why we missed the damage was obvious, it was still dark when we landed and we just hadn't looked. We were obviously leading a charmed life already.

The crew were indeed starting to ride their luck and yet they were only one-fifth of their way through their tour of operations. How long could their luck last? The year came to a close but what a year it had been for Les and his colleagues. His memories of the sunshine and beaches of South Africa seemed a lifetime away, although it had been just twelve months. However, there was no time to dwell for too long on the past, but to the relief, of all within Bomber Command, there were no operations on New Year's Eve and for one night at least there was some more time to relax.

Les amongst colleagues at the end of his final year at the Sunderland School of Pharmacy, 1939. Les is stood at the back eighth from the right.

New recruits in new uniforms at the Air Crew Reception Centre, August 1941. Les is second from right.

No 5 Initial Training Wing at the Templestowe Hotel, Torquay, Devon in December 1941. Les is standing in the front row, second from the left.

THE AIRCREW ASSOCIATION

(SOUTHAMPTON BRANCH)

Portrait of Les whilst at the Initial Training Wing as featured in an Aircrew Association publication.

Les at Berlin Railway Station in the Eastern Cape Province, South Africa in April 1942.

Ready for a game of tennis in uniform! South Africa 1942.

Course 6 Air Bombers at No 42 Air School, Port Elizabeth, South Africa in November 1942. Les is standing in the back row, second from the right; sadly, half of the course would not survive the war.

End of the course photograph and ready to return to the UK for whatever came next, March 1943. Back row (l-r): Les Bartlett, Charles Rousseau (killed aged 23 serving with No 429 (RCAF) Sqn, 24 March 1944, buried Kiel War Cemetery Germany), Sam South, Chick Roberts (died in May 1944), Ernest Greenwood (killed serving with No 83 Sqn, 25 April 1944, buried Durnbach War Cemetery Germany), Al Pardoe (killed aged 22 serving with No 61 Sqn, 20 February 1944, buried Hanover War Cemetery Germany), Geoff Roddis. Centre row (l-r): George Waters (killed serving with No 57 Sqn, 6 January 1944, buried Poznan Old Garrison Cemetery Poland), Dennis Whitley, Peter Gillard (killed aged 22 serving with No 44 Sqn, 10 May 1944, buried Evreux Communal Cemetery France), Peter Smith (killed in July 1946), Harry Wilson, Kiwi Shand, Padre Barber. Front row (l-r): Ron Jackson, Duncan McLean, Dinky Parry (killed serving with No 620 Sqn, 27 September 1943, buried Hanover War Cemetery Germany), Jerry Parker (killed serving with No 467 (RAAF) Sqn, 10 May 1944, buried Lezennes Communal Cemetery France), Taffy Jones, J. Fairburn (killed in air collision, June 1944).

Les at home on leave, 1943.

Bombing-up for another night of operations.

Les' office in the nose compartment of the Lancaster.

The crew's navigator, Frank Swinyard, trying out the rear turret during a daylight training sortie, 1943.

Below: The corkscrew was effectively the best way to deter an enemy fighter and often a crew's last chance manoeuvre.

Steep dive to Port

Climb to Starboard

Roll over

Steep dive to Starboard

Climb to Port

Roll over

The Kaiser Wilhelm Church in Berlin, taken before and after the bombing offensive.

The Beetham crew with their ground crew soon after their arrival at Skellingthorpe in late 1943. Having taken this photograph, Les does not appear but his crew colleagues are Sgt Fred Ball (far left), F/O Mike Beetham (second from left), Sgt Don Moore (fourth from left), Sgt Jock Higgins (third from right), Sgt Reg Payne (second from right) and P/O Frank Swinyard (furthest right).

The original Beetham crew at Skellingthorpe, late 1943 (l-r): Sgt Fred Ball (air gunner), Sgt Les Bartlett (bomb aimer), F/O Mike Beetham (pilot), P/O Frank Swinyard (navigator), Sgt Reg Payne (wireless operator), Sgt Don Moore (flight engineer) and Sgt Jock Higgins (air gunner).

No.50 Squadron Battle Order – 22nd November, 1943. BERLIN

	Pilot	F/Eng.	Nav.	A/B.	WO/AG.	MU/G.	R/G
A	F/O Pocovy	Sgt. Smith	F/O. Puggtt	Sgt. Bedingham	Sgt. Olson	Sgt. Kelbrick	Sgt. Ballanty
B	F/Lt. Balt..	Sgt. Brown	F/O. Matson	F/Sgt. Forrester	Sgt.	Sgt. Moody	F/Sgt. McDougal
C	P/O. Heslendorf Henderson	Sgt. Dale	F/O. Kewley	Sgt. HoPe	Sgt. Hall	Sgt. Turner	F/Sgt.
D	F/O. Beetham	Sgt. Moore	P/O. Swinyard	Sgt. Bartlett	Sgt. Payne	Sgt. Higgins	Sgt. Ball
E	F/Sgt. leader Rossenburg	Sgt. Condy	F/O Stevens	F/Sgt. Lewis	Sgt. Tulman	Sgt. Coulson
F	P/O. Litherland Green	Sgt. Scott	F/O. Hartley	Sgt. Harris	Sgt. Crawford	Sgt. Gross
G	P/O. Wilson	Sgt. Felton	F/O. Billam	Sgt. Newman	Sgt. Gunn	F/Sgt. Harrington	Sgt. Baker
H	Sgt. Lloyd	Sgt. Avenell	Sgt. Richardson	Sgt. Dewhirst	F/Sgt. Hewson	Sgt. McCarthy	Sgt. Bacon
J	F/Sgt. Writti	Sgt. Jones	F/Sgt. Delaman	Sgt. Gleeson	Sgt. Taylor	F/Sgt. Williamson	F/Sgt. Kellaghi
K	F/Sgt. Thompson	Sgt. Laws	F/Sgt. Cha Daen	Sgt. Conlon	Sgt. Corbett	Sgt. Spiers	Sgt. Wyllie
				Front Gunner – F/Sgt. Bolton			
L	F/Lt. Burtt	Sgt. Taylor	P/O. Freeland	P/O. Haynes	F/O. Betty	Sgt. Parkman	Sgt. Brookes
M	F/Sgt. Keith	Sgt. Mitchell	F/O. Guthrie	Sgt. Bendix	Sgt. Morrey	Sgt. Brown	Sgt. Rawcliffe
N	F/Sgt. Cummich	Sgt. Burton	F/Sgt. Westerman	Sgt. Staunix	F/Sgt. Sockett	Sgt. Redgern
O	Sgt. Dibbin	Sgt. Cave	F/Sgt. Balmer	Sgt. Jackson	Sgt. Richard	Sgt. Dutomb	Sgt. Mason
P	F/O. Lundy	Sgt. Stevens	F/Sgt. Jordan	Sgt. Bignell	Sgt. Green	F/Sgt. Runkle	F/Sgt. Wilding
R	W/O. Saxton	Sgt. Fryer	F/Sgt. Jowett	F/Sgt. Rees	Sgt. Watson	F/Sgt. Zurm	F/Sgt. Oates
			2nd Navigator – F/Sgt. Crerar				
S	P/O. Adams	Sgt. Mickeley	Sgt. Rawcliffe	Sgt. Ward	F/Sgt. Crawford	Sgt. Hastie	Sgt. Pillett
T	P/O Herbert	Sgt. Russell	Sgt. He	P/O. Bacon	Sgt. Poole	P/O. Hughes	Sgt. North
N	P/O. Weatherstone Gregory	Sgt. Thompson	F/Sgt. Lane	Sgt. Spruce	Sgt. Linehan	Sgt. Collingwo

O.C. Night Flying..........S/Ldr. W.F. Parks, DFC.
Duty Engineer.............Sgt. Brown.

R McFarlane
Wing Commander, Commanding,
50 Squadron, Skellingthorpe

No 50 Sqn Battle Orders for the Berlin operation on the night of 22/23 November 1943. The Beetham crew are shown listed fourth and this was their first of ten visits to the Big City.

ACTUAL LOSSES ON EACH OPERATION
(FIGURES TAKEN FROM
THE BOMBER COMMAND
WAR DIERIES

Year 1943		Aircraft			DUTY (Including Results and Remarks)	Time in Air				
						Observer		Gunner		
Month	Date	Type	No.	Pilot		Day	Night	Day	Night	LOSSES
			DV 217	F/O BEETHAM	CARRIED FORWARD	118.40	75.50	14.50		
NOV	19	LANCASTER			DINGHY SEARCH — SHOT DOWN 3 DEC 43, FRANKFURT	4.05				1
NOV	22	LANCASTER	VN "D" JA 899	F/O BEETHAM	N.F.T — SHOT DOWN 24 JUNE 44	.25				
NOV	22	LANCASTER	JA 899	F/O BEETHAM	"OPS" 1st BERLIN		7.15		26	2
NOV	23	LANCASTER	JA 899	F/O BEETHAM	"OPS" 2nd BERLIN — LANDED WITTERING FLAPS U/S		7.45		20	3
NOV	24	LANCASTER	JA 899	F/O BEETHAM	WITTERING - BASE	.35				
NOV	26	LANCASTER	DV 376	F/O BEETHAM	"OPS" 3rd BERLIN — SHOT DOWN BERLIN 15 FEB 44. DIVERTED MELBOURNE		8.05		28 +14 UK	4
NOV	28	LANCASTER	DV 376	F/O BEETHAM	MELBOURNE - BASE	.20				
					13 LANCS FROM 50 SQ TOOK PART. 7 RETURNED ONE LOST OVER GERMANY AND 5 CRASHED IN U.K.					
					SUMMARY OF FLYING TIMES FOR NOVEMBER	11.40	37.45			
					TOTAL DAY HOURS	132.55				
					TOTAL NIGHT HOURS		98.55			
					MW Beetham. F/O					
					CAPTAIN					
					Mitchell F/Lt FOR S/L O.C 'A' FLIGHT					
						118.05	98.55	14.50	74 + 14	

CRASHED DURING TAKE-OFF AND LANDING

Page from Les' log book for November 1943.

Heading for Berlin, taken by Les soon after take-off at dusk.

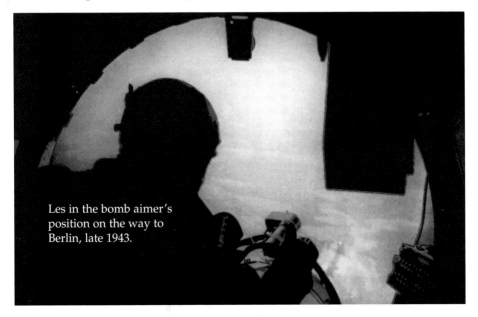

Les in the bomb aimer's position on the way to Berlin, late 1943.

Les trying out
the controls
during a
daytime
training sortie.

The winter of 1943/44 at Skellingthorpe was a particularly hard one, not only due to the operational tempo against some of Germany's most heavily defended targets but also because the weather in Lincolnshire did not make life any easier. The aircraft shown is LL744 VN-B (or VN-Beetham as it became known), the Beetham crew's trusted mount during January 1944. The crew took this aircraft on ops twenty times.

No 50 Sqn dispersal at Skellingthorpe, January 1944.

Whilst this photograph from Les' diary makes a nice winter picture postcard scene, it also highlights the difficulties faced by the ground crew during January 1944 to keep Skellingthorpe operational; the great efforts by all the station personnel at Bomber Command bases across the east coast of England often goes unrecognised.

Les in flying equipment at Skellingthorpe.

Les' aiming point photograph for the aircraft assembly plant at Marignane near Marseille, 9 March 1944.

Les as a newly commissioned pilot officer at Skellingthorpe, March 1944.

Lancaster bomb bay showing a 4,000lb HC impact-fused 'Cookie' surrounded by 500lb GP bombs. One of the ground crew is giving a final check before take-off.

Les' aiming point photograph for the aircraft factory at Toulouse, 5/6 April 1944.

Les' aiming point photograph for the Juvisy railway marshalling yards, 18 April 1944.

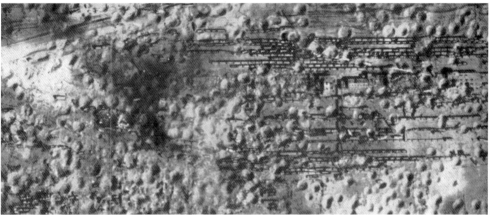

Bomb damage to the marshalling yards at Juvisy, 18 April 1944.

The Beetham crew taken towards the end of their tour of operations at Skellingthorpe, April 1944 (standing l-r): Sgt Jock Higgins (air gunner), F/L John Blott DFC (air gunner), F/L Mike Beetham DFC (pilot), F/O Frank Swinyard DFC (navigator), P/O Les Bartlett DFM (bomb aimer). Sitting (l-r): F/O Ted Adamson (flight engineer) and Sgt Reg Payne (wireless operator).

Friday, June 30th, 1944.

BILLINGHAM MAN WINS D.F.M.

A GALLANT AIRMAN

Has Many Exciting Experiences

Pilot Officer Les Bartlett of Billingham, R.A.F.V.R. 50 Squadron, has been awarded the D.F.M. for gallantry and devotion to duty on air operations. He operated with his squadron as Flight Sgt. Bomb Aimer, and took part in attacks as far apart as Stetin on the Baltic coast and Marseilles on the Mediterranean, having done ten trips to Berlin, also Liepzig, Stuttgart, Brunswick, Nuremburg, Schwinfurt, Frankfurt, Essen and other targets.

He has had many exciting times —the most exciting being when abandoning aircraft by parachute —two of the crew were killed.

Before joining up, Bartlett was a chemist and druggist and worked at Moffitt's, Station Road, Billingham.

He is an old boy of Stockton Secondary School and of Constantine College, Middlesbrough. He volunteered as a pilot and was re-mustered as Bomb-Almer in South Africa. He wears the 1939-43 star His wife and daughter reside at Eckford By-pass Road, Billingham. Co DURHAM

Les and Margaret outside Buckingham Palace after receiving his DFM from the King on 31 July 1945.

Local newspaper cutting back in County Durham covering the award of the DFM to Les.

Les and colleagues during the winter of 1944/45 whilst instructing on No 1654 HCU at Wigsley.

Les and colleagues in Berlin during the first of his 'flag-waving' trips to Berlin, October 1945. Post-war politics saw Berlin divided into four sectors and the four main powers were keen to present a strong visible presence in Berlin.

Les whilst serving at Thornaby during early 1946.

Les standing on one of Berlin's reinforced concrete flak towers, which had been built as part of the city's defences, October 1945. Les was amazed to find the flak tower intact despite the surrounding area being totally devastated.

Les' wartime pilot remained in the post-war RAF and rose to command at the highest levels. Here, MRAF Sir Michael Beetham GCB CBE DFC AFC is shown escorting the Queen Mother.

Les shortly before being demobbed in 1946.

Les (left) and Sir Michael at one of their many gatherings.

The Nos 50 & 61 Squadrons' Association Memorial on the former site of RAF Skellingthorpe. Les was actively involved on the Memorial Committee to raise the money for this marvellous memorial and it was unveiled by Les' wartime pilot, MRAF Sir Michael Beetham GCB CBE DFC AFC, on 3 June 1989.

The three surviving members of the Beetham crew at the annual re-union held on the former site of RAF Skellingthorpe (l-r): Reg Payne (wireless operator), Sir Michael Beetham (pilot) and Les Bartlett (bomb aimer).

Les' medals showing (l-r): Distinguished Flying Medal, 1939-45 Star, Air Crew Europe Star, Defence Medal, 1939-45 War Medal.

The white silk scarf worn by Les throughout his tour of operations now hangs proudly in his lounge.

Les Bartlett DFM at a reunion more than sixty years after the war.

CHAPTER SEVEN

A New Year
But The Same Old Story

The first night of the new year began with another raid against Berlin. Harris sent an all-Lancaster force of 421 aircraft to attack the city but the target was again cloud-covered, which made the task of marking the aiming points difficult; consequently, bombing was scattered. Losses were relatively high: twenty-eight Lancasters were lost. For Les it had been a long evening. The sortie time was eight hours and fifteen minutes, which was his longest to date. In his first seven operational sorties he had already been to Berlin and back five times. Clearly he was feeling the strain of operational life on a bomber squadron.

Saturday-Sunday 1–2 January 1944

My 5th Berlin. No report from me, I'm too tired.

Not only was there the stress of operating deep into the heart of Nazi Germany, but there was also a hard winter back at base. As 1944 began, the weather at Skellingthorpe took a turn for the worse.

Tough as it was on operations over Europe in the winter, I was pretty sure that we were as likely to fall victim to the elements as we were to lose the nightly battle with

113

the *Luftwaffe*. Lincolnshire is very flat and well known for the hard winters it suffers. Apart from the almost continuous fog there is the biting wind which blows in from the North Sea across the Wash bringing snow more often than not. This seemed bad enough if you were lucky enough to be stationed at one of the many peace-time stations like Waddington, Coningsby and Scampton. They were all built in the 'thirties to very high standards, but to be stationed at one of the satellites of these base stations was no picnic. At Skellingthorpe, accommodation consisted of Nissen huts and prefabricated buildings. When it was wet the unmade paths were a sea of mud, and when it was cold IT WAS COLD! We shared a Nissen hut with the NCOs of another crew. It was pretty grim. In the centre of the hut was a solid fuel stove from which, when we had fuel for it, you could only feel the heat if you were less than 2ft away. We had a meagre allocation of coke, which didn't last long, but as it happened we were sited next to the coke compound and the 8ft high wire fence was frequently scaled in the dead of night for extra supplies. There were periods of prolonged frost, which resulted in all the pipes in the communal section being frozen. This had diverse effects on each individual. Some thought it was a good excuse not to wash or shave, and some of the more ambitious were able to get organized for a bath in various ways.

Although the crew was very much involved with operations, there were also the occasional training sorties. This would keep the crew active and would also provide opportunities to practise new navigation and bombing techniques, as well as providing airborne tests of aircraft systems or equipment following any maintenance carried out on the aircraft. The improvements in technology also meant that new equipment was being introduced into service at a rapid pace, particularly on the Lancaster during 1943/4. The number of training sorties varied from crew to crew but using Mike Beetham's crew as a typical example, the ratio during January 1944 was a training sortie for every two operations flown; they were typically in the order of one to one and a half hours long.

Les's next operational sortie provided the crew with another new name on their target list. The raid against Stettin on the night of 5/6 January 1944 was the first major attack against the city since 1941. Now called Szczecin, and part of Poland since the end of the Second World War, the city is situated on the Baltic Sea to the north-east of Berlin. It was an important large port for the Germans as well as being of tactical importance for the eventual advance of Russian ground forces from the east. At over eight and a half hours' flight time there and back, it was a long way to the target but was a familiar route for the crew. A diversionary attack by Mosquitoes against Berlin helped confuse German defences and the raid produced reasonable results, including the sinking of several ships in the harbour. For the Beetham crew it was a long night.

Wednesday 5 January

Tonight it is Stettin, the last trip before the full moon period. We took off just before midnight in 'F-Freddie'. The night was wizard; bright moonlight enabled us to see what was going on for a change. We got into the main stream just as we crossed the coast and there were kites all over the place. The first leg was a bind; instead of having 30 miles of sea to cross it was 300 miles. It was nice and quiet; we did not see a thing while crossing Denmark although Sweden put up a little light stuff bursting at 15,000ft. I presume that was to show their neutrality – we did go very close to their Baltic coast. It was wonderful to see their coastal resorts all lit up. After living in the 'blackout' it was like a glimpse of fairyland.

When about 30 miles from the target the moon

disappeared and left us in the dark. We settled down to bomb and I did a 'bang on' run up on the centre of the city. The raid was highly concentrated and kites were bombing above, below and on all sides of us. Visibility was excellent and I could clearly see whole areas of houses and shops blasted and blazing like an inferno. The place burned furiously and made such a glare that the exit from the target was like an arena. I could see Ju88s and Me110s all over the place, six in one direction and four in another. We were in the last wave and they had got wise to us by then. I saw a Ju88 climbing rapidly from underneath a Lancaster on to its tail and pause there. His guns must have either jammed or he was out of ammo because he didn't fire a shot, nor did the Lanc. I don't think they even saw him! We were lucky as we weren't even picked on so we 'stooged' out and climbed up to 25,000ft.

Coming back from Stettin we ran into bad weather. We were still in the top layers of a warm front and visibility was almost zero. We had two narrow squeaks, both with Lancasters. The first Lanc suddenly crossed above us from port to starboard and nearly took our mid-upper turret with it; the second just appeared on the port beam and before we knew where we were he was blazing away at us, how he didn't shoot us down I can't imagine, it was point blank range. Gradually we left the cloud behind and got back over the Danish coast. By this time at 25,000ft dawn was breaking but by travelling west we were not letting it catch us up and when we crossed the Yorkshire coast it was still half light. It was great to see the countryside again, the canals and locks of Lincolnshire, the smoke and haze over the old city. At 0825 hrs the wheels touched the deck and we heaved a big sigh of relief. To say we were tired was putting it mildly; we had done a round trip of 1,700 miles and it had taken us eight hours and forty minutes, which is longer than the average Berlin trip.

There were no major raids for Bomber Command during the following week and Les had to contend with just one practice bombing sortie on 10 January. For his next major effort, Harris chose the city of Brunswick on the night of 14/15 January. Situated in the northern part of Germany, about 100 miles south of Hamburg and 100 miles west of Berlin, this historic city had been a focal point in the region for the rise of the National Socialists during the early 1930s. Tactically, its importance was centred on being part of Germany's rail network but otherwise, Brunswick was a relatively small and less important target as far as the overall bombing strategy was concerned and had not previously been visited by Bomber Command.

The Beetham crew was one of nearly 500 Lancaster crews that took part in the operation. The route to the target was a long transit over the North Sea before coasting in over the Bremen area. The German night fighters were able to hassle the main force all the way to the target and on the return transit until the bombers coasted out over Holland. As far as the bombing was concerned, there was only minimal damage to the southern parts of the city. Many bombs also fell on smaller towns to the south of the target. Losses were relatively high with thirty-eight Lancasters lost on the raid (nearly 8 per cent of the force dispatched).

The Brunswick raid was not a success. In the overall strategic campaign, it was not considered an important enough target and Harris would only periodically send his bombers back to the city, and even then in smaller numbers. For Les, the Brunswick raid was just over five hours airborne and it was his shortest raid to date. The entry in his diary, however, suggests he was very tired.

Friday 14 January

Brunswick – no report from me.

There followed a few days of no activity before Harris decided to return to Berlin on the night of 20/21 January. This was the first raid against the capital for more than two weeks and marked the beginning of a third phase of operations. From Bomber Command studies it was apparent that less than 25 per cent of Berlin had been devastated, less than the damage caused to other major cities at that time. For example, Hamburg was estimated to be 70 per cent devastated, Wuppertal the same, Mannheim and Hanover 55 per cent, Düsseldorf and Essen 40 per cent and Dortmund 33 per cent.

Therefore, to increase the pressure against Berlin, Harris decided to bring more aircraft into his plans so that an increasing amount of tonnage could be dropped on the city. This required an increased involvement from the Halifax squadrons, which up until that time had only been used in any considerable numbers on two of the ten raids. He also had more Mosquitoes available and more Pathfinder Lancasters were now equipped with H2S.

The Beetham crew, once again, featured on the operations board. Although they did not know it at the time the next forty-eight hours were to be extremely busy and extremely tiring. At 769 aircraft, the force dispatched to Berlin on the night of 20/21 January was the largest against the capital to date and the largest main force assembled since the Battle of Hamburg six months earlier. The northern route to the target gave the German defences time to prepare and the night fighters were once again able to hassle the bomber stream, both inbound and outbound. The target area was covered in cloud, which made the Pathfinders' task of sky-marking difficult. That said, the PFF appeared to mark the target successfully but it was not possible to assess the bombing results achieved.

Thursday 20 January – (My 6th Berlin)

By all accounts this was going to be a big bashing. We took off in daylight at about 1630 hrs and reached the Dutch coast almost before it was dark. We went in just north of Heligoland this time, and they had a good bang at us. The rest of the journey was pretty quiet. We should have been in the fifth wave but by some error (question-able) in navigation (sorry Frank), we got there with PFF and bombed as the attack opened. There were bags of fights just outside the target area and I saw two Ju88s get a Lanc each. All the fighters seemed to be at least 2,000ft below us, which was a good thing. On the return journey a Lanc had a belt at us but missed – must have had trigger twitch badly – apart from that nothing much happened. We came back like nobody's business and were third back in the circuit. There were no squadron losses.

The following night, 21/22 January, it was back to Berlin once more. Although the main effort of 650 aircraft was against Magdeburg, the Beetham crew was one of twenty-two Lancasters and ten Mosquitoes tasked to carry out a diversionary raid against Berlin. Situated less than 100 miles to the south-west of Berlin the city of Magdeburg was considered to be an important part of the rail network. The combination of its close proximity to Berlin, and being *en route* to the city, proved to be disadvantageous to the Bomber Command crews. Unsurprisingly the German controllers did not work out that Magdeburg was the target until very late but they were still able to position the night fighters in the right area to cause the main bomber stream considerable problems. Fifty-seven aircraft were lost (nearly 9 per cent of the total force). The majority of the losses were Halifaxes, more than 15 per cent of those dispatched, and most of these are believed to have been to night fighters. As far as the diversionary raid to Berlin was concerned, one of the Lancasters was lost.

This raid was the first major raid against Magdeburg, although by the end of the war it suffered considerable damage and became the second most devastated city in Germany; only Dresden having suffered more. The very impressive Gründerzeit suburbs in the northern part, called the Nordfront, were totally destroyed, as was the main street with its Baroque buildings.

Friday 21 January – (My 7th Berlin)

This was something new to us. Two kites from our
squadron, ours and one other, had to join No. 617 and 57
Sqns to do a feint attack on Berlin to draw off the fighters
from the main bomber force which was to attack
Magdeburg. We went with the main stream as far as
position 'C', which was halfway between Hanover and
Berlin, then we carried on to the 'big city' while the main
force turned due south. Actually, we were briefed not to
run unnecessary risks to bomb the centre of the city,
because our main task was to create the impression that
the main force were heading that way.

On the approach to the target at 22,500ft we found the
flak very spasmodic and half-hearted, so in we went to
the centre of the searchlight belt and, bang on ETA [esti-
mated time of arrival], we bombed. Cloud obscured the
ground but we saw a series of flashes as the bombs burst
and the rear gunner reported the glow from a huge fire
as we left. We were the first aircraft to bomb – PFF being
about thirty seconds late; 'Beetham does it again', now
for home! We were given a specified time to reach a
certain position on the Baltic coast and being about seven
minutes early we did two complete orbits outside Berlin.
While doing so we noticed Magdeburg, the main force
target that night, getting it hot and strong. Towards the
end of the attack there were hundreds of fighter flares all
around and it was as bright as day there. Everything was
quiet until we crossed over the Swedish and Danish
islands in the Kattegat, then all hell broke loose; the flak
was almost as bad as Berlin. Mike weaved like mad and
led the Jerry radar one hell of a dance. Nothing much
happened after we got over the North Sea – now it was
just a two-hour bind back to base.

Visibility was bad, height and cloud bases about
9,000ft but we got down OK, so why worry? Well, No. 50
Sqn did it again – sixteen kites, no early returns, no losses

and only one kite damaged – 'A-Able'. It was shot up in a fight; one engine packed up and the port tyre burst but P/O Toovey did a good landing so everything was OK.

There were a few days rest before the Beetham crew were on their way back to Berlin. Bomber Command's next major raid was on the night of 27/28 January, when Harris ordered a force of more than 500 Lancasters against Berlin with several more diversionary and support operations. The diversionary operations had some success and fewer night fighters managed to hassle the main stream. Once over Berlin the crews found the area covered by cloud and bombing was spread over a large area. Thirty-three of the Lancasters were lost.

Thursday 27 January – (My 8th Berlin)

Tonight, like it or not, it is our thirteenth trip and our eighth on the 'big city'. Take-off time was 1630 hrs. That's the way we like it, getting airborne in daylight, giving us time to get into a good solid stream before it is dark. On this operation a maximum effort was made to confuse the enemy defences as to our route and target. We went in north of Cuxhaven and made for Hanover. Flak and fighters were moderate. I saw only two aircraft shot down during the whole night. We then turned south in an attempt to make the enemy think our target was not Berlin. The success was questionable because approaching the target the usual mob of night fighters was in evidence. Much to my surprise, these 'Jerry' fighters were throwing caution to the wind. Instead of 'stooging' round the outskirts of the target area they came tearing in amongst their own flak. On our actual bombing run we were attacked three times and each time I left my bombsight to man the front turret. The main force was so concentrated that I saw many Me109s and Ju88s 'stooging' about, not being able to decide which

Lanc to attack. It was spasmodic however, as I learned back at base, because aircraft which bombed before and after us saw no fighters at all over the target.

The way home was supposedly safe, but very long and boring. We first skirted Leipzig and made for the outskirts of Frankfurt. Here they picked us up and fighters were dropping groups of flares continually along our track. Isolated aircraft were shot down on this leg but we weren't attacked at all, and crossed the French coast with the marker beacons of Beachy Head clearly visible. We seemed to cross the Channel in no time and gradually little coloured lights were appearing all around us as each aircraft decided it was out of the danger area and switched on its navigation lights. Weather conditions were by no means ideal. We had to make for the Wash to get through low cloud with comparative safety, and found at least ten aircraft in the base circuit area below 1,000ft! However, two circuits of the 'drome and it was our turn to come in. As the landing was rather hurried I had no time to leave the bombing compartment and go aft as I should have done. However, Mike did a wizard landing and everybody was happy.

There was to be no rest whatsoever. After just a few hours' sleep the Beetham crew had to go to nearby Waddington to pick up a Lancaster. When they returned to Skellingthorpe they found out that they were on operations again that night. The target was again Berlin. This raid on 28/29 January, was Les's fourteenth and his ninth to Berlin. It was effectively a maximum effort involving 677 aircraft: 432 Lancasters, 241 Halifaxes and four Mosquitoes. For Les it would prove to be an unforgettable night. The route took the main force over northern Denmark, which was beyond the range of most German night fighters. Instead they were waiting over the target area and forty-six of the bombers were lost. Once over the target there were breaks in the cloud, which meant that the Pathfinders were able to use ground-marking techniques.

Bombing was concentrated and there was significant damage to the city.

Friday 28 January – (My 9th Berlin and 14th Operation)

Although we didn't get to bed until 0430 hrs we had to get up at 0900 hrs to go to RAF Waddington to collect a Lanc, the rest of the squadron being able to stay in bed until lunchtime. On return to base we went straight to the mess and found we were down again on the operational list so the usual procedure was followed; briefing was tannoyed for 1415 hrs, and we found that it was Berlin once more. Things were rather uncertain at flight planning, and although everything was prepared, take-off time was not decided, but provisionally fixed for 2345 hrs. Of course, we all intended to get about three hours' sleep in the mess during the evening, but the inevitable card game started and we played until 2130 hrs, following up with an operational supper of ham and eggs.

At 2230 hrs we donned our flying gear, got transport out to the aircraft and passed a leisurely hour doing final checks on engines and equipment. There is none of the usual glamour attached to a midnight take-off compared with a daylight flight. However, as we passed flying control, we did get a friendly, unexpected Aldis. Dead on time we raced down the runway and were airborne, the night was crisp and clear and aircraft could be seen in all directions circling round to enable them to set course from base. The first leg was long and tedious, taking over an hour, but the sight of heavy flak as we passed north of Heligoland broke the monotony. We met the first opposition as we crossed the Danish coast not far from Flensburg. Searchlights were more active than usual, showing through a few very large breaks in the clouds, but PFF were on top form and had put down our route markers very accurately, enabling us to keep to definite areas. PFF also provided the first two casualties. Shortly after crossing the coast two full loads were seen to drop or be jettisoned by the crews as their aircraft went down. Ten-tenths cloud again gave us maximum cover, tops being up to 22,000ft, making it difficult for either fighters or ground defences to pick us up. This situation, however, only lasted as far as Rostock, where all medium and high cloud dispersed, leaving a clear sky and just a thin layer of stratus near the deck.

Then the fireworks started. We were about 40 miles from the target and the familiar red Very signals from fighter to fighter were everywhere in the sky. As we were in the fifth wave of the attack practically the whole of the main force was ahead of us and I could see combats taking place in every direction. Luckily for us the majority were 3,000 to 4,000ft below us. By the time we got to the target the enemy fighters had laid a flare path right across our track from west to east, we actually saw a Ju88 coming flat out dropping these globular flares at intervals of about 1,000 yards making the whole area as bright as day. The attack was in full swing and, as I gave Mike alterations of course to get the target in my bomb sights, I could see numerous huge fires and one particularly vivid explosion which seemed to light up the whole of Berlin with a vivid orange flash for about ten seconds. At the critical moment I yelled the now familiar 'Bomb doors open', followed by 'Bombs gone', and 'Bomb doors closed.'

It was then just full steam ahead. Just as I was making my usual checks to ensure that there were no bombs left hung up, Mike yelled, 'There's a fighter ahead attacking a Lanc.' It was a Ju88. Before the words were out of his mouth I was up in the front turret blazing away. After this for about thirty seconds it did a slow turn to port then spiralled down to earth. From then on we were alert and I stayed up in the front turret for about twenty minutes until we were out of the target area. The fighters were, no doubt, up in strength but none of those we saw came within range and we assumed our normal routine.

On our way back and about 50 miles from the target, I discovered I had a 500lb bomb 'hung up', and at the same time, through a break in the clouds, I could see the lighting system of a German aerodrome – most likely a night-fighter station. So I threw the jettison bars across and much to our delight a few moments later out went the lights on the ground. The next source of annoyance proved to be the coastal defences of Lubeck. They threw up plenty of well-predicted heavy stuff, which necessitated about a quarter of an hour of good evasive action on the part of Mike before we cleared the area.

From then on over the Baltic and Denmark we saw absolutely nothing but occasional short bursts of flak – no fighters or searchlights at all. Out to sea we went, to let down slowly this time, there being one hour and fifty minutes left in which to descend before we reached base. A clear broadcast picked up by Reg gave us news that the cloud base was down to 800ft and we had to exercise great caution making sure exactly where we were before we attempted to break cloud. This we did and much to our surprise we came in from the sea over the coast at Skegness – thanks to Frank, our navigator. From there to base we did in the half light of dawn at low level, landing at base at 0840 hrs feeling very, very tired and very hungry.

The Combat Report for this raid, which was submitted by the squadron to HQ No. 5 Group, read as follows:

From: No. 50 Sqn, Skellingthorpe.
To: Headquarters, No. 5 Group.
Date: 29 January 1944

Ref: 20S/470/Arm.
Combat Report

On the night of 28/29th January 1944, Lancaster 'B' of No. 50 Sqn, was detailed to attack Berlin. At 0323 hrs, on the bombing run, position target, height 21,300ft, speed 146 rectified, on a course of 100 magnetic, a Ju88 was sighted by Captain on Starboard down, and rose to ahead, crossing from Starboard to Port at 500 yards. The front and mid-upper gunners both opened fire allowing 1 1/8 rads deflection, strikes were observed. 'B'-50 executed a corkscrew to starboard and enemy aircraft flew down on the Port beam. The Ju88 is claimed as damaged. Monica did not indicate.

Weather clear.
Front gunner – 50 rounds.
Mid upper – 100 rounds.

Captain	F/Lt Beetham
Engineer	Sgt Moore
Navigator	P/O Swinyard
Air Bomber	Sgt Bartlett
WOP/AG	Sgt Payne
M.U. Gunner	Sgt Higgins
Rear Gunner	Sgt Ball

Signed:	Flight Lieutenant A. Gray, Gunnery Leader
Signed:	Wing Commander T.W. Chadwick, Commanding No. 50 Sqn, Skellingthorpe.
Signed:	Group Captain D.D.Christie, Commanding RAF Station, Skellingthorpe.

Immediately after this raid, the Beetham crew were given a few days leave. They were now almost halfway through their tour of operations and had survived fourteen operations, nine of which had been against Berlin. January 1944, in particular, had been a busy month, nearly sixty hours of operational night flying at an average of eight hours per sortie. There was much to look forward to and Mike Beetham's recent promotion to the rank of flight lieutenant had added to the crew's high spirits.

Aircrew on operations were normally given seven days' leave every six weeks during their operational tour; this, of course, was not always possible. For those that did manage to get their leave, each had his own preferred way of spending his valuable time with loved ones or simply getting away from it all. One way of getting away was known as a Nuffield Break. Lord Nuffield, the famous motor manufacturer and industrialist, had set up a scheme whereby aircrew, at no expense to themselves, could get away with their wives to spend their leave at one of a number of hotels around the country. Les decided to take up this opportunity to spend some valuable time with Margaret. His diary records the few days in early February.

I chose the North British Hotel in Edinburgh for Margaret and me. That was about as far away from London as you could get. We found another aircrew couple had arrived before us and on arrival we started to compare notes. All was not well! The residents at the hotel were mainly Scottish clansmen and their wives.

At dinner on the first night we chose from a menu which was offered to us. It was wholesome but not in the least bit exciting. Perhaps because we were on an operational station we were used to a rather high standard of food. I must admit we always had eggs and bacon for a 'flying meal' before an operation and frequently had eggs for breakfast whereas eggs were a rather scarce commodity off the station. Anyway, after dinner that evening we four got our heads together and made a plan of action for the following night. When the waiter came to our table we turned down the offer of a menu and pointing to the next table I said, 'We would like the same as they are having.' That brought a look of horror on the waiter's face. 'Oh that is Lord and Lady So-and-So and they have their food sent in from their estate in the Highlands.' On looking around it was apparent to us that the same applied to everyone in the dining room except us. So we were stuck with our braised steak and potatoes boiled in their jackets. Just to show our resentment however, the following night we each walked into the dining room with a pint of beer. That DID cause some strange looks.

The next night the four of us decided to try our luck at a local fish restaurant. It was full of sailors from the nearby port of Leith. As we were being served with our meal a fight broke out between two adjacent groups of sailors. Chairs were flying left and right and I just shouted, 'Let's get out!' We were about 50 yards away when the waiter came tearing up the street shouting, 'You haven't paid!' My reply was, 'We haven't eaten either – get lost!

The following night we went to the popular dance hall in Edinburgh – the Plaza I think it was called. There we were in for a shock. As we went up to the pay box two burly naval police proceeded to frisk us. I was surprised but Margaret was quite shocked at the thoroughness and roughness with which it was done. Apparently knives were a popular accessory in Edinburgh during the war. Nevertheless, we had a very enjoyable evening dancing to the local maestro. So ended our break. We said goodbye to our new-found friends and the following morning we were on the train; Margaret back to her home in Billingham and I was on my way back to my squadron.

CHAPTER EIGHT

On The Edge

Les and his colleagues returned from leave on 7 February and, as normal, the first hours were spent catching up on news of what the squadron had been up to and what each of the crew had done during their few days off. Since Les had left Skellingthorpe there had been a further major effort against Berlin on the night of 30/31 January but not much else. The first week of February had seen Bomber Command conduct a number of minor operations and there was to be no major effort during the second week of the month either, and so the first few days back at Skellingthorpe were quiet.

Monday 7 February

Returning from leave we found another crew living with us in our Nissen hut. 'What happened to the previous crew?,' we asked. Nobody knows. We suspect the worst.

Tuesday 8 February

Did some practice bombing at Wainfleet and flew back in formation with P/O Lloyd.

Wednesday 9 February

More practice bombing at Wainfleet.

Thursday 10 February

Mess party tonight, too much control exercised and everyone ended up pretty sober. A few 'odd bods' managed to get tight; Fred, our rear gunner, was trying to play the double bass the last I remember of him. I later heard he slipped and put his foot through the big drum.

Friday 11 February

No flying today, weather duff.

The following day Saturday 12 February 1944, was to be a day the crew would never forget. There were no operations for the squadron that night and so the Beetham crew was programmed for local fighter affiliation training with a Spitfire during the afternoon. Soon after lunch they prepared themselves in the normal way for a training sortie and then walked out to their aircraft, W4119 'VN-Q'. At 2.45 p.m. the crew took off from Skellingthorpe. The events that followed are best told in Les's words.

Saturday 12 February

This is a day I shall never forget. I undoubtedly owe my life to my parachute. At 1445 hrs we took off in VN 'Q-Queen', closely followed by a Spitfire. We had our crew of seven, plus P/O Jennings and his two gunners, and the detail was called 'fighter affiliation'. It was agreed that Mike should fly for twenty minutes with our gunners giving commentaries on the attacking Spitfire, then we should turn around and P/O Jennings take over while his gunners manned the turrets. Having changed pilots and gunners, I was standing with my head in the astrodome watching the fighter come in to make its first attack on the homeward leg, when the flight engineer shouted over the intercom, 'Port outer on fire!'

I turned quickly, saw flames and heard the pilot shout, 'Feather the engines and cut off fuel!' This had no effect, however, so I grabbed my 'chute and made my way down the kite over the main spar to the rear door, where I plugged into the intercom just in time to hear the pilot shout, 'Abandon aircraft quickly!' 'Bomb aimer jumping,' I replied, and without further ado I fixed my parachute pack on to my harness, whipped off my helmet, opened the rear door, pegged it back and out I went.

I distinctly remember having no sense of falling whatsoever and when I could no longer hear the roar of the engines I pulled the ripcord. With a crack like a whip my 'chute opened, my harness took the strain and my fall to earth was checked. From then on I seemed to be just suspended in a void and not descending at all. I looked all around to take stock of the situation; the earth was blotted out by 10/10ths cloud, and I was 7,000ft above it. Far ahead, at least 2 miles away, I could now see the kite still flying but gradually going into a steeper dive. At this point – and not until – the second parachute appeared, and this was promptly followed by numbers three, four and five. Number six, however, did not appear, for a reason which I shall explain later. It turned out that Reg was second, Jock third, Mike fourth, Frank fifth and P/O Jennings sixth.

The kite then disappeared into cloud and I looked around. Two Lancasters appeared and were circling round me and waving 'like the clappers' so I returned the wave and off they went. I later learned that one of them was being flown by an old pal of mine from 61 Sqn who was stationed with us at Skellingthorpe. Suddenly, everything was foggy. I was in cloud and my 'chute was whistling and flapping with the opposing wind currents. In a short space of time I was through the cloud layer and the earth began to creep up to meet me. At 1,000ft I realised that I was heading for a canal. Wearing no 'Mae West' and not being able to swim, I tugged frantically at the appropriate side of my 'chute and cleared it with yards to spare. However, my troubles were not over for there, directly below me, were high-tension cables. How I missed them I do not know, because, when lying on the ground, I was right beneath them. They distracted my attention so much that I did not prepare myself for touching down and I hit the deck with a hell of a bang. The ground, however, was a ploughed field and thankfully cushioned my fall.

Well, things began to happen. As I stood up and released my parachute harness, two farmers came running up with shotguns, apparently taking no chances in case I was German. I raised my arms and shouted 'RAF, RAF!' After that a mixed gang of kids came running up, all firing questions at me as fast as I could listen to them. Between them they argued about who would carry my parachute and one fellow settled it by carrying it himself. Needless to say I was highly excited, having escaped with my life. I was thrilled. I remember singing on the way down. I found out later that was also the case with three other chaps. Well, my first concern was to get in touch with base, so I enquired for the nearest 'phone. This turned out to be in the village doctor's house, only 50 yards away.

By now all the villagers of Revesby [a village near the airfield of Coningsby in Lincolnshire] were out and I felt quite a hero as they walked up the street with me. At the doctor's house the housekeeper answered the door. She looked at me as though she was seeing a ghost – I suppose my muddy appearance, together with yards and yards of parachute trailing behind me, was rather a strange sight. I was invited in and removed my flying boots, leaving them at the door to avoid a mess. The old girl made me tea and sandwiches while I got through to base on the 'phone. My 'gen' certainly shook the Wing Co. He even rang me back to repeat everything because it all sounded so fantastic. At this point a boy rushed in shouting, 'Mister, you had better get out quickly, the women outside are going to cut up your parachute!' so I brought it inside for safety. I then had tea, and only after it was pointed out to me by the doctor, did I see that there was a huge lump on my forehead about the size of an egg caused by my parachute harness bumping my head as my parachute opened up. Boy! – was it good to relax in a chair again? I was as stiff as hell, the inevitable result of the stretching you get when your 'chute opens.

After the tea and sandwiches, I cleaned my flying boots and had a walk down the road. It was difficult to realize the drama that had been enacted up in the quiet and peaceful sky; it all now seemed a far-away dream. At 1830 hrs transport arrived from RAF Skellingthorpe to pick me up. The 'gen' was that others of the crew were at RAF East Kirkby where they landed, so off we went to pick them up. You can just picture me throwing my arms around Jock, Reg, Frank and Mike and each firing questions at each other. Then I heard the worst, Fred the rear gunner and Don the flight engineer had gone down with the kite, as also had P/O Jennings's two gunners. That was bad – what a blow to their families!

On our way back to base, as the miles went by, I gathered the rest of the story from the boys. As I left the kite, Jock arrived at the door and saw everybody crowding round just watching me going down, then after bags of hesitation on everyone's part Jock decided to jump. This is just as it should NOT be done. Firstly, he did not remove his helmet and he went out with his intercom trailing after him; he also took a running jump instead of rolling out from the Lancaster step, consequently he hit the tail plane with a hell of a bang and thirdly he pulled his ripcord as he went out. So there he was straddled across the tail plane with his 'chute trailing after him. However his 'chute had eventually pulled him over the top edge and he sailed away safely. This episode was witnessed by all at the rear door and, no doubt, put them off considerably. Reg's last memory is of Fred standing in the door with his parachute clipped on, looking as white as a ghost and, having obviously lost his nerve, he wouldn't jump.

By this time the kite was losing height rapidly and to quote Reg's words, 'I dived out.' Much to his dismay he found that, although he was pulling like mad, his 'chute didn't open and he was down to 2,000ft before he realized he was pulling the canvas carrying handle instead of the ripcord handle. Luckily he pulled the right handle in time and no sooner had his 'chute opened than he touched down. As he did so he saw a wing on fire come sailing down like a falling leaf as the rest of the kite hit the deck. It apparently crashed on the perimeter track of East Kirkby aerodrome and wrote off another Lancaster. Of the kite and the poor chaps inside, little was recognizable and it was only with difficulty that the victims could be identified among the debris of the fire.

Frank, Mike and P/O Jennings apparently made the jump from the front escape hatch in the floor of the bombing compartment and found it quite easy. When we reached Skellingthorpe we first went into the mess. What do you think? The WAAF waitress dashed up and started kissing and hugging us. We had no idea how popular we were in that mess. Then a meal – ham, eggs, chips and fried bread, my favourite meal – as Joyce, the waitress, well knew.

It was now 2230 hrs and from then on until midnight we did some good solid 'line shooting' to a mess full of those on duty – and they loved it. The MO spoiled our fun; he rolled up and insisted that we got to bed as quickly as possible and gave us some tablets to make sure we slept. He even ran us to the billet in the ambulance to make sure we got there!

So ended the most exciting day of my life! The last thing I remember was gazing at my ripcord handle. I had the presence of mind to hang on to it as I descended. The

WAAFs in the sick quarters thought we were worth keeping in, they even tried to persuade the MO to admit us for three days' rest, unfortunately without success.

The loss of Don Moore and Fred Ball was a tragic blow to the crew at a time when they were halfway through their tour of operations. The loss was deeply felt by each member. They had been together for some time and had got to know each other so well. How ironic it was that Don and Fred had been to Berlin and back nine times only to lose their lives over Lincolnshire, just a few miles from their base, during a training sortie. Four of the crew, including Les, carried Fred Ball's coffin at his funeral in Birmingham and Frank Swinyard went to London to attend Don Moore's funeral.

For the surviving members of the crew, the following few days were spent getting over their ordeal and, even in wartime, there was the inevitable inquiry to determine the cause of the crash; particularly as there had been loss of life.

Monday 14 February

Had an easy day today and paid a visit to the parachute section. I presented the WAAF who packed my parachute with the usual ten-shilling note. (You could say, 'Cheap at twice the price.') The crew were given forty-eight hours' leave to get over the experience. I feel that this is an appropriate time to pay tribute to the WAAFs of the parachute section who do a tedious job packing and repacking our parachutes. Only on the rare occasion, when an accident happens, do they realize that saving lives is what it's all about. We certainly proved that the parachutes worked. My thanks to the packers – we are eternally grateful to them!

Wednesday–Thursday 16–17 February

Today was the Court of Inquiry about the crash. Mike attended. Reg, Jock and I were given a forty-eight hour pass to celebrate our survival, so Reg took us to his home in Kettering, where Jock walked into a lamp post outside the Rising Sun and split his nose! As you can guess, he was a serious drinker!

Friday 18 February

Went to Fred's funeral in Birmingham. It was a grand affair but as he was a Roman Catholic we didn't understand much of the service.

As replacements for Don Moore and Fred Ball, the crew were joined by Pilot Officer Frank Adamson, flight engineer, and Pilot Officer John Blott, who was the squadron's Gunnery Leader. Red-headed and a former boxing champion John Blott was widely respected by his peers and superiors alike. He had joined the squadron in June 1943 and had already distinguished himself during the Battles of Hamburg and Berlin. On the same day that he joined the Beetham crew his award of the DFC was confirmed in the *London Gazette*. He had been strongly recommended for the award after completing twenty operations, during which he had damaged at least two enemy fighters and had always shown courage and a strong enthusiasm for opening combat with enemy fighters at the earliest opportunity. By the time his DFC had been confirmed, he had just completed his own tour of operations but he volunteered to join the Beetham crew for the remainder of their tour.

And so after a break of three weeks for various reasons, the Beetham crew returned to operations on the night of 19/20 February. For the target Harris chose the city of Leipzig. This was a familiar target for the crew as they had been there before, back in the early days of December, although it must have seemed like years rather than weeks before. The crew took their aircraft, LL744, for its routine NFT on the morning of 19 February. The flight lasted just thirty minutes and was the first time that the crew had been airborne since their recent ordeal.

The raid was a maximum effort with a total force of 823 aircraft, which consisted of 561 Lancasters, 255 Halifaxes and seven Mosquitoes. It proved disastrous for Bomber Command. The wind forecast was inaccurate and German night fighters were continually attacking the main force all the way to the target. Once at Leipzig, the bombers found the target area covered by cloud, and several arrived early (including the Beetham crew) and had to wait for the Pathfinders to mark the target. This led to some mid-air collisions amongst the main force and losses due to flak. A total of seventy-eight bombers were lost, which represented nearly 10 per cent of the force dispatched. Worst hit were the Halifaxes, which suffered thirty-four aircraft lost (more than 13 per cent of the Halifax force), with several more having to turn back. This raid proved to be the last operational appearance of the Halifax Mk II and Mk V.

Saturday 19 February – Leipzig – My 15th operation

The Wing Co. wasn't wasting much time! 'Get Beetham's crew airborne!' At 1000 hrs we were up on our NFT. We all felt as calm as ever after our baling out incident. We took off at 1800 hrs and it was a 'twitchy' trip right from the beginning. We had dense cloud to get through and bags of icing up, but we were lucky and found a break. From the moment we crossed the coast it was a battle, kites were going down left and right. To make matters worse the winds changed and we got there far too early and had to do orbits outside Leipzig waiting for zero hour. The trip back was just the same. The next day we heard the score – seventy-eight aircraft lost, although none were from No. 50 Sqn. What a price to pay!'

Sunday 20 February

I awoke to hear the tannoy calling all crews to the briefing room. Here we go again! You can imagine our joy to find we are not on tonight. F/Lt Short is going instead and taking our Lancaster 'B-Baker'. Bomber Command went to Stuttgart and only lost a few kites – what a contrast to the previous night!

Thursday, 24 February

Tonight it was Schweinfurt but we were not on. Hooray! Lincoln, here we come!

Having been off the squadron operations board for the last couple of raids, Les and the crew found themselves back there on 25 February for the night's raid against Augsburg. First, though, they had to fly another crew down to Barford St John in Oxfordshire, which was the satellite airfield for Upper Heyford, to recover one of the squadron's aircraft that had landed there during the night of the Schweinfurt raid. It was a short trip, and the crew had the rest of the afternoon to prepare for the night ahead.

Augsburg was deep in the heart of Bavaria, in southern Germany, and had first been bombed by Lancasters in a famous low level-raid in broad daylight on 17 April 1942, led by Squadron Leader John Nettleton and involving just twelve Lancasters, six from No. 44 Sqn and six from No. 97 Sqn. They had attacked the Maschinenfabrik Augsburg Nurnburg diesel engine factory, causing considerable damage to the factory, which resulted in disruption to the production of diesel engines for several weeks, but proved costly for Bomber Command, seven of the twelve Lancasters were lost, although John Nettleton was awarded the Victoria Cross for his outstanding leadership during the raid.

The raid against Augsburg nearly two years later was quite a different story. A force of nearly 600 bombers took part in the raid on the night of 25/26 February, and the widespread bombing caused considerable destruction across a large area. The weather over the target was clear and defences were light as Augsburg was not considered by the Germans to be of high importance to Bomber Command. This led to most bombs falling on the target area, causing considerable damage to various factories and buildings, although the raid later caused controversy due to excessive damage to the historic centre of the city. Losses to Bomber Command were relatively light with only twenty-one aircraft lost. At eight hours duration, it was a long round-trip.

Friday 25 February – Augsburg

We did an NFT in 'A-Able' and took a crew down to Barford St John, near Upper Heyford, to pick up 'K-King', which had landed there from Schweinfurt. We got back at lunch-time and, after a quick lunch, went to briefing. Augsburg was the target in Bavaria. Take-off was 1835 hrs and we got airborne OK; cloud base was 2,000ft so we were in cloud almost immediately, although not for long. At 6,000ft we cleared the tops and it was beautiful above. We saw a lovely sunset on the starboard beam as we set course for the coast. We were well on time too, almost the first aircraft to break cloud. Soon we saw Lancs breaking through here, there and everywhere, and the main force formed up into a good solid stream in no time. Our first defect was the intercom in the rear turret. It was very intermittent and although Reg took the gunner, John Blott, a spare helmet, it didn't remedy the trouble, but we carried on. When crossing the Channel Jock got violent stomach pains and it was touch and go whether we should return to base. Jock said he'd stick it out though, and did. Apart from two or three little battles and some flak the next thing worthy of mention was the glimpse we got of the towns in Switzerland as we flew along the Swiss/German frontier. They were naturally all lit up and they looked like fairyland way down below us.

By this time the target was coming into view, we could see the defences of Munich and Augsburg clearly, hundreds of searchlights and bags of flak. They looked keen until we got over them. Then, as the bombs went down, their morale seemed to go to the dogs; the flak eased up and the searchlights just swerved here and there. What a prang! The place was burning from end to end. As we left, clouds of smoke filled the sky. Then the worst happened – my oxygen tube came adrift and I passed out. Mike, getting no reply from me, sent the engineer, (now F/O Adamson), down to the bombing compartment to investigate. He fixed up my oxygen tube and it was about half an hour before I was really myself again. Even then our troubles were not over. The oil pressure in the starboard outer dropped so we had to shut down the engine. In spite of that we managed to get back on three and Mike made a wizard landing back at base. When we got to debriefing the press was there, what a line we shot! – well, just a little. That's what they came for wasn't it?

The next major effort ordered by Harris was against Stuttgart on the night of 1/2 March; again, the Beetham crew were involved. The main force consisted of 557 aircraft, including 415 Lancasters. The route was cloudy and the crews found no change over the target area. It was, by recent standards, a quiet night with the weather conditions preventing the German night fighters from penetrating the main force; only four aircraft were lost. At over eight hours duration it was another long round-trip for the crew.

Wednesday 1 March – Stuttgart

Nice southern route, it was the quietest trip we have ever done. We didn't even see one combat or a single cannon shell. We got back to base OK and found the losses to be low. Good show!

The next few days proved to be quiet but frustrating for Les as operations were planned and then cancelled.

Saturday – Monday, 4–6 March

The most binding time I have ever experienced. Each day we got 'ops gen'; tested the kite, bombed up, briefed, dressed and then went out to the kites and then it was scrubbed. Two Munichs and a Keil escaped – lucky them! The first night we all went to Skellingthorpe village and got drunk, but we couldn't afford to do that every night – not like our wealthy allies, the Yanks.

Although there were no operations for the crew during the first week in March, it was not an uneventful week. On the 7th, Les and his colleagues took the Commanding Officer of No. 53 Base, RAF Waddington, Air Commodore Arthur Hesketh, flying on a training exercise. As Skellingthorpe was a satellite base of Waddington, this gave the crew a chance to spend some time with their commanding officer. Then, just two days later, Les received confirmation of his appointment to a commission as a pilot officer. He had not been a flight sergeant for long but his personal qualities had impressed his chain of command and he had been recommended for a commission. His diary records the event as just a simple entry.

Thursday 9 March

As a result of my interview with Air Vice-Marshal Cochrane, OC No. 5 Group at Group HQ, Morton Hall, Lincoln, my commission to Pilot Officer was announced today at Station HQ RAF Skellingthorpe.

Celebrations, however, would have to wait as the crew were detailed for operations that night. The target was not to be the normal run across to Berlin, or some other target deep inside Germany, but something very different. They were detailed to attack an aircraft assembly plant at Marignane, near Marseille on the south coast of France. This raid was to be different for several reasons. Firstly, it was the first time the crew was to attack a target in France. Secondly, because it was in France, the raid required precise bombing and so the crew would release their bombs from 10,000ft, which was well below their normal bombing height in excess of 20,000ft, and in bright moonlight conditions. Thirdly, they were to be part of a small force of just forty-four Lancasters from No. 5 Group and not a large main force. For Les, as a bomb aimer, raids such as this were unlikely to come around very often and he was full of excitement.

Thursday 9 March

Tonight we reap the benefits of all the practice flying we have been doing for the past few nights, to ensure that this trip was a success. The show really started at 1000 hrs when bomb aimers, instead of going out with their crews to do the necessary ground tests on their aircraft, went to the bombing section to study closely and memorize all available photographs and maps of the target, which was a Ju88 night-fighter assembly plant. Apart from that, flight planning and briefing was carried out in the usual way but with more secrecy than ever before. I'm getting excited – precision bombing for a change.

The operational meal was at 1700 hrs and to look round the mess I think it was obvious that the crews were rather concerned as to the outcome of this raid; after all it was a full moon tonight and it was very different to be one of forty-four aircraft instead of several hundred. The thing which upset the boys most, I believe, was the fact that we were definitely told it would be impossible to return to base, as visibility would be down to 1,000 yards. Of course we were given an aerodrome in the south-west of England which could take us on return, but that's not the point. One always likes to get back to base after operating.

Towards dusk, visibility rapidly decreased and we

began to wonder if we should even be able to get airborne, but luck was with us and precisely at 2000 hrs we taxied on to the flare path and took a last long look at the lights of the aerodrome, which immediately became lost in the fog as we became airborne. The first hundred miles or so were most uninteresting. First we had to climb through this layer of fog, which took about half an hour, and from then on for the rest of the trip we were in brilliant moonlight. We didn't see the south coast of England because of fog. The same applied to the coast of France, but we knew we were over France because the defences of Le Havre were banging away at a kite which was evidently off track.

About half an hour later things began to get more interesting. We usually bombed from 20,000ft to 22,000ft but from the height of 10,000ft, which was the height for this special operation, I could easily see French towns and hamlets, rivers, roads, railways etc. I passed my information on to Frank to aid his navigation. Soon the ground below us began to rise and everything was snow-bound as far as I could see. These were the foothills of the Alps, and being only 1,000ft below us in places, they gave us the impression of travelling at great speed. At one point we were passing over the ground so fast that I remember asking Mike if we were going to clear the peaks at that height without climbing a little.

Once across the Alps, it was apparent that we were reaching warmer regions, the snow disappeared and the land once more became flatter. Soon the Mediterranean coastline came into view. This is where my job really started. With the aid of my maps I ordered alterations of course to take us to our rendezvous. We contacted the other aircraft on the operation and circled around while Leader One called up his deputy leaders. This spot was supposed to be marked by a can of incendiaries, but due to a boob on someone's part they fell into a lake! It didn't matter, however, because visibility in the moonlight was so good I could easily fix our position. On receiving the order 'ONE GREEN' by R/T from the leader we proceeded to the target and circled it while it was marked with one red spot fire.

By this time the ground defences had tumbled to our target and searchlights and flak began to be a nuisance. Next came the order 'TWO GREENS', whereupon all aircraft in the first wave left the target area and proceeded to the 'pinpoint' which was the tip of an isthmus of land on a lake. From there we started a 'time and distance' run for bombing. Unfortunately, my bombsight was unserviceable so I had to make a rough estimation as to when to bomb, based on my theory of bombing! This proved to be 'bang on'. I could not have done better with a serviceable bombsight. We were first to bomb and my bombs straddled the target, the three hangars of Marseilles Marignane airport. Simultaneously I got a wizard photograph of the aiming point. I felt like shouting, 'Go home boys – the target has gone!' I didn't, of course. That would have been a breach of R/T discipline.

That was that – now it was 'Bomb doors closed' and away we went climbing to 12,000ft as instructed, circling around while the second wave bombed. This took approximately another three minutes, then came the much awaited order from the leader 'TWO YELLOWS', which was the signal to set course for home. My last glimpse of the target showed it to be in a very sad state. The whole area was clouded over with smoke and dust; fires, too, had started from the incendiaries which had been showered down by the last two aircraft.

Then there came the long and tedious flight home – only once did we see anything that looked at all suspicious. It was a twin-engine kite (friend or foe?) stooging along 1,000 yards ahead of us, obviously not having seen us, so there was no cause for alarm.

Eventually back at base it was good to hear that

friendly WAAF voice saying, 'OK PILGRIM "B-BAKER" NO. 1 PANCAKE.' In no time our wheels were down on the deck with engines cut and we were piling out. So ended the longest trip we have ever done. Nine hours in the air on twelve Horlicks tablets, two packets of chewing gum, ten fruit drops, one bar of chocolate, a flask of coffee and a handful of 'wakey-wakey' tablets.

As Les mentioned in his diary, it was the crew's longest sortie to date and it would, in fact, remain the longest of the tour. The raid proved a success and no aircraft were lost. Today, the site is Marseille-Marignane Provence Airport and during 2000, Les returned to Marseilles to see how the attack was reported by the *Provence Presse*. A search of the news archives produced no report whatsoever; it seems most likely that the German news censors did not wish to publish any details. However, the local journalists were delighted to meet Les and were keen to hear what memories he had of the raid. He spent four days in Marseilles being interviewed by journalists from the *Provence Presse* and by the secretary of the Chamber of Commerce where the city archives are kept. A photographer took pictures of his log book and an article about the raid appeared in the newspaper the following day.

Following the Marignane raid, the crew were given a few days' leave. Whilst they were away the squadron commander recommended the DFC for both Mike Beetham, as captain of the crew, and Frank Swinyard, the navigator. The citation for Mike Beetham's reads:

On the night of 3/4 December 1943, the aircraft of which he was captain was attacked by a Ju-88 after leaving the target. The port centre petrol tank was holed and much fuel was lost, but due to his skilful handling he managed to reach this country and land safely. Then, on the night of 25/26 February 1944, he was captain of an aircraft detailed to attack Augsburg. Shortly after leaving the target, the starboard outer engine failed. Once again, Flight Lieutenant Beetham proved his skill and brought the aircraft safely back to base on three engines. He has always shown a high standard of efficiency and has proved himself an excellent captain of aircraft. For his consistent devotion to duty, his gallantry in the air, and the offensive spirit which he has shown in battle, he is awarded the Distinguished Flying Cross.

Not only were there recommendations for Mike Beetham and Frank Swinyard, but also for the award of the Distinguished Flying Medal (DFM) for Les Bartlett for his success during the eighteen operations flown to date and for damaging a night fighter during the raid against Berlin on the night of 28/29 January. The Marignane raid had been his first operational sortie as a commissioned officer and his tour up until then had been flown as a sergeant and flight sergeant. Therefore, the recommendation was for the DFM rather than the DFC awarded to commissioned officers.

The DFM had been instituted in 1918 and was awarded to non-commissioned officers and other ranks for an act, or acts, of valour, courage or devotion to duty performed whilst flying in active operations against the enemy. It is a most attractive-looking award, oval-shaped and silver. On the obverse is the sovereign's effigy and on the reverse is Athena Nike seated on an aeroplane with a hawk rising from her right hand above the words 'FOR COURAGE'. The medal is surmounted by a bomb attached to the clasp and ribbon by two wings. The ribbon was originally thin horizontal violet and white alternate stripes but from 1919 the stripes run at an angle of forty-five degrees from left to right. All awards are verified in the *London Gazette*. A total of 6,637 DFMs were awarded during the Second World War, which was considerably less than the 20,354 DFCs awarded to commissioned officers for similar acts of bravery.

Les Bartlett's citation for the DFM, dated 15 March 1944, was as follows:

F/Sgt Bartlett is the Air Bomber in the crew captained by F/Lt Beetham and has now completed 18 successful sorties against such targets as BERLIN (9) Leipzig, and Augsburg. During his tour he has proved himself a most competent and efficient bombadier. On the night of 28/29 January, 1944 he was in an aircraft detailed to attack BERLIN. Whilst the aircraft was over the target it was attacked by a Ju88. On hearing the gunner's warning F/Sgt Bartlett promptly manned the front turret, and as the enemy aircraft broke away after making its attack, F/Sgt Bartlett opened fire from the front turret. His shots were seen to strike the Ju88 and this aircraft was claimed as damaged. The majority of targets which he attacked had been obscured by cloud but he obtained photographs of the aiming point at Augsburg, Stettin and Marignane. He has always shown the greatest desire to operate and his determination to get his bomb on the target in spite of heavy enemy opposition has always been outstanding. For his devotion to duty and courage he is recommended for the award of the Distinguished Flying Medal.

With Les's commission confirmed, and a DFM to come, it was just reward for a particularly tough tour of operations so far with eighteen operations already under his belt, nine of which were to Berlin. Away from the operational scene, Margaret was expecting a baby. And so, when Les went home on leave in March 1944 there was much to look forward to. It was just a matter of surviving the remainder of his tour of operations!

CHAPTER NINE

Not Berlin Again!

aving returned from nine days' leave, Les felt ready for anything. Whilst away there had been one raid against Stuttgart on the night of 15/16 March and two against Frankfurt on 18/19 and 22/23 March; all three of these were large-scale efforts and each involved well in excess of 800 aircraft. There was no time for the crew to settle back; they found that they were immediately on the squadron's battle orders for their first night back.

The weather forecast for the night of 24/25 March 1944 described the midnight frontal position as a feeble warm front from between about 60N 003E and 55N 005E (over the North Sea) becoming colder down towards the Frankfurt area and across to Vienna. Fog was forecast to develop at 3 a.m. in Lincolnshire and East Anglia and from 4 a.m. in Yorkshire. The forecaster predicted that all Bomber Command groups would have at least half of their bases available until 2 a.m. with visibility at the airfields of at least 1,500 yards. Across Germany there was forecast to be a belt of stratocumulus along the front. To the east of the front there would be patchy medium cloud and little or no low cloud. East of 015E, on the Baltic coast, there would be broken stratocumulus and good visibility. Over Berlin the forecast was a good chance of clear skies but there was a possibility of 10/10ths thick stratocumulus. There was a better prospect of good weather in the Brunswick area. The forecast over France was generally little amounts of cloud with some patchy stratocumulus in the north-east.

For his main effort, Harris chose Berlin with diversionary and support operations at Kiel, Munster, Duisburg and airfields in the Low Countries. For Les and the crew, and for 810 more crews across Bomber Command, it was to be Berlin – the crew's tenth visit to the 'big city'. The official Bomber Command Report of Night Operations (Night Raid Report No. 562) for the night of 24/25 March 1944 gives both historians and enthusiasts alike a good insight into the planning and overall statistics for the raid. Whilst not particularly special, nor in any way unusual, this report provides a good example of a Bomber Command maximum effort, particularly against Berlin, at that stage of the war.

The plan for this raid was for the main force to take the northern route out to the target and then return by a more southerly route, in a clockwise direction. This meant that once off-target bombers were never turning back into others that were inbound to the target. Looking at the route in more detail, the northern route took the main force out eastwards across the North Sea. Once on the eastern side of Denmark, it turned south-east across the Baltic Sea, whilst staying north of the Kiel area, and then coasting in around Rostock. Having coasted in over northern Germany, the main force maintained a south-eastwards heading passing to the north of Berlin and then making one final turn south-west to attack the city from the north-east. Off-target, the bombers maintained a south-west heading until well clear of Berlin. The return route then passed between the defended areas of Hanover and Leipzig before turning north-west towards Holland, passing well clear of Hanover to the south-east. Once over Holland the route took up a westerly heading direct for base.

The method of attack planned for the Pathfinders was complicated but was essentially Newhaven with emergency sky-marking. The blind marker illuminators were to drop green TIs and white flares blindly if there was less than 7/10ths cloud. If there was more cloud then the plan was to release green and R/P flares (red with yellow stars). If H2S was unserviceable then all markers were to hold their TIs and flares and bomb with the supporting aircraft. Visual markers were to mark the exact aiming point with mixed salvos of reds and greens. Those blind 'backers-up' detailed to attack before 'z + 7' (where 'z' is the time of the first main force bombers on target) were to aim at the centre of all the TIs, if Newhaven was in progress. However, if cloud had prevented this then they were to drop markers blindly. Later arrivals were to drop both reds and sky markers blindly. Visual 'backers-up' were to aim reds at the centre of the mixed salvos, or at the centre of all TIs, with a two-second overshoot. Supporters were to bomb blindly, if possible; otherwise after visual identification or on good dead-reckoning (DR) if at the centre of all TIs, or sky markers on a heading of 217 degrees magnetic.

Instructions for the bomb aimers of the main force were less complicated. The main force bombers were to aim at the centre of all mixed salvos in the early stages of the raid and at the centre of the reds at the later stages of the raid. If TIs could be seen then the main force was to bomb the centre of the sky markers on the same heading of 217 degrees magnetic.

The timing of the attack was for 'zero' hour to be at 10.30 p.m. and the duration of the attack was to last from 10.25 p.m. (the time of the first blind marker illuminators) until 10.45 p.m. (the time of the last bombers overhead the target). The total attacking force was, once again, to be in excess of 800 aircraft. The total force can be broken down as follows: twenty-eight blind marker illuminators (to mark at 'z − 5' minutes); six visual markers to mark at 'z − 3'; twenty blind backers-up to mark between 'z − 1, and z + 14'; twenty visual backers-up to mark between 'z' and 'z + 14'; and seventy supporting aircraft to be available from 'z − 5'. The main force of over 650 aircraft had just fifteen minutes to complete its attack: 125 aircraft to bomb between 'z' and 'z + 3'; the next 125 aircraft to bomb between 'z + 3' and 'z + 6'; 128 aircraft to bomb between 'z + 6' and 'z + 9'; 125 aircraft to bomb between 'z + 9' and 'z + 12'; and the last 129 aircraft to bomb between 'z + 12' and 'z + 15'.

A further twenty-six Airborne Cigar (ABC) aircraft were to

be used throughout the attack. These Lancasters from No. 101 Sqn at Ludford Magna carried an additional crew member (a special duties operator) and were equipped with the highly secret Airborne Cigar equipment, which was designed to jam German night fighter communications frequencies. As a diversion, eleven Mosquitoes were to drop 'window' ahead of the main force over Denmark and then bomb Kiel. These aircraft were to drop four bundles per minute from 53N onwards and two bundles per minute once off the target area.

Window had been one of the simplest yet most effective devices produced during the war. The basic principle involved strips of aluminium foil which, to radar systems, produced a response similar to that of an aircraft. Therefore, thousands of strips would produce thousands of radar responses, which caused confusion to the German defences. Tactically it was used one of three ways: to simulate an entirely separate bombing force; to cause confusion to defences when splitting from the main force at a pre-determined point, or to saturate an entire area such as the Ruhr to disguise the exact target.

For the Berlin raid of 24/25 March, the diversionary Mosquitoes were also detailed to drop spoof fighter flares to the south-west of Berlin. In addition to the window dropped by the Mosquitoes, the main force were also required to drop two bundles of 'window' per minute once within 50 miles of Berlin, and one per minute for the rest of the route. As a further diversion, a force of about 150 aircraft from the various operational and training units were to fly to within a few miles of Paris while the main force was on its way to Berlin, although they were not to drop any bombs.

With the planning and briefings over, a total of 811 aircraft were eventually despatched to Berlin. The actual weather experienced *en route* to the target was 9–10/10ths of strato-cumulus with cloud tops at about 5,000ft out to about 007E. Thereafter the stratocumulus broke to small amounts and the sky was clear until Rostock, after which the cloud then increased to 6–9/10ths and became variable towards the target. Over the target there was variable stratocumulus of between 2–9/10ths, with cloud tops about 5,000–6,000ft and moderate visibility. There was no moon. On the southerly return route the cloud dispersed from about 20 miles south-west of the target and there was no further cloud until west of Holland. Back at base the stratocumulus had mainly dispersed over Lincolnshire but persisted further east. As forecast, the visibility at the airfields slowly deteriorated but most remained fit until 3 a.m. but not, as it would turn out, No. 50 Sqn's base at Skellingthorpe.

It was generally not the cloud that caused problems, but the wind. At their operating altitude of around 21,000ft, the crews found the wind speed to be more than 60 knots from the north during the transit and more than 100 knots from the north over Berlin. This was considerably stronger than fore-cast and resulted in the bombers being blown south during the transit. The main bomber force became scattered as crews struggled to remain on track and on time. The conditions also made marking the target difficult with markers being carried beyond the target. The overall result was that scores of towns and villages to the south of Berlin recorded bombs falling in their area, although a large number of bombs did fall in the south-western parts of the capital. The plot of night photographs taken by the crews showed that all the bombing was well to the south-west of the intended target area.

The wind continued to cause problems during the return transit and many strayed too far south and came under attack from the defences that the route had been so carefully planned to avoid. Of the 811 aircraft that took part in the raid, 660 reported attacking the primary area and twenty-six attacking alternative areas. There were fifty-three aborts and seventy-two aircraft were lost (nearly 9 per cent of the force despatched). Les's diary records the night's events.

Friday 24 March – (My 10th Berlin)

Having just returned from nine days leave I was feeling fit for anything, but not for long. 'Ops' are on tonight and we are on the Battle Orders, they don't waste much time in this place. Over lunch we discussed possibilities for the target. With a heavy fuel load it must be a long trip but no one seemed to fancy Berlin because it looks as though the Yanks have taken over and are doing daylight raids. Still, that was all wishful thinking because when we got to briefing it was, 'Yes, Berlin again boys' – and to crown everything Met says clear skies over Germany. This wasn't good news and we all more or less got the 'twitch'. It's bad enough flying in cloud and bad visibility at 22,000ft but clear skies? That's another 'kettle of fish'!

At 1900 hrs we took off and set course over the North Sea for a point off the German coast. That is where our troubles started. The winds were so variable and instead of passing the northern tip of Sylt we were all over the place and some of us got a real pasting with flak over Flensburg. The next leg took us across Denmark, then down to the Baltic coast. Many chaps got into trouble here with the defences of Kiel, Lübeck, and Rostock. I saw at least four kites go down in a very short space of time. We had a near squeak at Rostock, the wind blew us into their defences and we were coned by four or five searchlights. After a few violent manoeuvres Mike managed to shake them off before the flak got the range. They were very tense moments for us.

Once Rostock was left behind, it was straight on to Berlin and with a 100mph wind behind us we were there in no time. Luckily, over the target, a thin layer of stratus cloud had formed which made it difficult for the searchlights to pick us up, so we hadn't much trouble on the bombing run. Shortly afterwards, however, things got hot. The enemy fighters put a ring of flares down across our path as we were leaving the target area. Luckily, although we saw a few fighters, none attacked us and all we had to do was to dodge the flak and keep out of the defences of Leipzig, Brunswick, Osnabruck and Hanover. Along this leg we saw bags of combats, and kite after kite went down in flames so we were absolutely on the alert and ready for anything.

The worst didn't happen however, and we cleared the Dutch coast safely with a little cloud cover to help us. Back at base they had problems too. Fog again became dense and we received a message from base to say that it was out of the question to try and land there so we were to divert to Docking in Norfolk. We found the place OK and got safely into the circuit with the rest of the squadron. We were given No. 6 to land, but this was our unlucky night. We were circling around the 'drome waiting to come in when No. 3 pranged on the runway so landing was out of the question. We were given an alternative to make for RAF Coltishall. Mike was cheesed off by this time and when the first aerodrome lighting system came into view he called them up and we got 'OK B-Baker pancake'.

It turned out to be RAF Fiskerton. We landed with the aid of 'FIDO' which was a system used when fog made landing difficult. There were large pipes along each side of the runway into which petrol was pumped and set alight and you landed between these two sets of flares which ran the whole length of the runway. It looked rather daunting when in the circuit but to Mike it was no problem. We were glad to get down and our flight commander landed behind us. It wasn't until the next day that we found that although Bomber Command losses were high, all of our squadron got back safely. Three cheers for No. 50 Sqn!

The following day the crew made the short flight back to Skellingthorpe and was relieved to find out that they were not on operations that night. The raid against Berlin on the night of 24/25 March 1944 would prove to be the last against the capital during what later became known as the Battle of Berlin; indeed, it was the last major raid of the war against Berlin, although the city would continue to be attacked by small numbers of Mosquitoes.

The Battle of Berlin lasted from mid-November 1943 until the end of March 1944, although there had been three earlier raids against the capital during a two-week period from late August to early September 1943. There had been sixteen major raids during the period 18/19 November 1943 to 24/25 March 1944, totalling more than 9,000 sorties with nearly 30,000 tons of bombs dropped. The Battle of Berlin proved to be the longest and most sustained bombing offensive of the Second World War and cost Bomber Command more than 500 aircraft. No. 50 Sqn had suffered forty-five aircrew killed on the Berlin raids alone during the winter of 1943/4. Combined with No. 61 Sqn's losses during this same period, RAF Skellingthorpe had suffered 123 aircrew killed against Berlin alone.

The Beetham crew's next operation was just two nights later, against Essen on the night of 26/27 March. This was the crew's twentieth, and their first against Essen. By comparison with the rest of their tour, it was a 'short hop'. Essen was in the heart of the Ruhr close to other industrial towns and cities such as Düsseldorf, Duisburg, Dortmund, Bochum, Krefeld, Mönchen-gladbach, Bottrop and Wuppertal. Because it was relatively close, it could easily be reached during the shorter nights of spring and summer and had been subject to attacks the previous year but, apart from the occasional minor operation, it had been left alone since the summer of 1943. Because of the close proximity of several industrial centres, the Ruhr defences were understandably very heavily concentrated. However, Harris's sudden change of emphasis from Berlin to Essen caught the German defences by surprise and the raid proved a success. Although there was cloud over the target, bombing was accurate and several industrial installations were destroyed or seriously damaged. Bomber Command losses were extremely light; nine of more than 700 aircraft despatched. As far as Les was concerned, it was a quiet night and there was nothing of note to write in his diary.

26/27 March 1944 – Essen

No report from me.

If the Essen trip had proved relatively uneventful, the next major effort by Bomber Command, against Nuremberg on the night of 30/31 March 1944, was to be a complete contrast; in fact, it would prove to be Bomber Command's most costly night of the war. As the winter nights were drawing to a close, Harris realized that his bombing offensive deep into the heart of Germany was coming to an end. Plans for the forthcoming Allied invasion of Europe were also reaching their final stage and he knew that it would not be long before his attention would be required elsewhere.

His choice of Nuremberg was an interesting one as it was an ancient city of no particular industrial importance. There were, however, a number of small factories around it and it was part of a central link in important rail and water communications. It was deep into enemy territory, way to the east of the southern part of Germany. Any route taken to the target would involve flying very close to heavily defended areas. There was much discussion over the weather forecast but the decision was made to proceed with the raid. Of the 795 aircraft despatched, ninety-five would fail to return (nearly 12 per cent of the force dispatched) and ten more were written off back at base. Bomber Command casualties were 535 aircrew killed and a further 180 wounded or taken as prisoners of war.

When analysing the raid, it appears that the weather forecast was wrong. Coupled with several wind-finding errors made by the crews, the main force became so scattered that 20 per cent did not pass within 30 miles of one turning point. This led to a straggling force of more than 100 bombers that bombed the town of Schweinfurt by mistake. The German night fighters also enjoyed considerable success and constantly harassed the main force throughout. It is reckoned that by the time the main force arrived at Nuremberg, some eighty bombers had been shot down with a further fifty-five having aborted for technical reasons. Furthermore, the crews found the target area covered by cloud and, as a result, bombing was scattered and little damage was caused; most damage was to the residential areas, with only a slight effect on industrial installations. For those that took part, including Les, it was a night never to be forgotten

Thursday 30 March – Nuremberg – (My 21st Operation)

Such a nice day today – little did we know what was in store for us. The usual 'ops twitch' was on at 1000 hrs. We went out to our Lancaster, 'VN B-Beetham', and did a ground run. Everything was 'bang on' as usual. Briefing was getting later each day as the days grew longer, and today it was at 1700 hrs so we all had an afternoon nap after lunch. The target was Nuremberg. 'Where's that? Bavaria. Oh, this should be a nice quiet stooge,' said someone. But was it? At 2200 hrs we taxied out from our pad and were No. 1 airborne, setting course after a wide circuit to gain height to 20,000ft over the channel.

At this height we crossed the enemy coast and it was eyes wide open – look out for trouble. As we drew level with the south of the Ruhr Valley things began to happen. Enemy night-fighter flares and their familiar red Very signals were all around us, and in no time at all combats were taking place and aircraft were going down in flames on all sides. This aggravated the situation because each time a kite hit the deck a great glow lit up the sky and night was turned into day, making it easier still for the enemy fighters to see us.

So serious was the situation that I can remember looking out at the other poor blighters going down and thinking to myself, Well it must be our turn next, just a question of time. Perhaps it will be that chap above us, or perhaps it will be us.' In the heat of the battle a Lancaster appeared on our port beam converging on a collision course, so we dropped a hundred feet or so to let him cross. He was only 200 yards on our starboard beam when 'crash' – a string of cannon shells hit him and down he went. The night fighter which got him must have been on our tail at the same time but with so much happening we didn't spot him.

At Position 'C' we altered course for Nuremberg and I looked down on the port beam at the area over which we had passed. It looked like a battlefield. There were kites burning on the deck all over the place – bombs going off where they had been jettisoned by bombers damaged in combat, and fires from their incendiaries across the whole area. Such a picture of aerial disaster I had never seen before and certainly hope never to see again. I suppose it was just the same on daylight raids except that the spectacle of a kite on fire at night is much more terrifying. On the way into the target the winds became changeable and we almost ran into the defences of Schweinfurt but altered course in time.

The defences of Nuremberg were nothing to speak of – a modest amount of flak which did not prevent us from doing a normal approach, and I was able to get the target indicators dropped by PFF in the sighting head of the bombsight. I scored direct hits with our 4,000lb 'cookie' and our 1000lb bombs and incendiaries. With our eyes peeled we were able successfully to get out of the target area, which is always a dodgy business, and set course for home. To reach the coast was a binding two-hour stooge. We saw a few combats so Mike did a banking search fairly frequently to make sure no enemy fighters were getting tucked in underneath us in order to deliver that fatal burst of cannon shells which the latest Ju88s were so good at. They had installed an upward-firing cannon and called it *Schräge Musik* – Jazz Music!

It was about this time the moon finally dropped below the horizon and we breathed a sigh of relief. But the varying winds were leading us a dance. We found ourselves approaching Calais instead of 80 miles south so we did a slight detour to avoid their defences. Once near the enemy coast it was nose down for home and we crossed out over the channel with 300 knots on the clock. Even then we saw some poor bloke 'buy it' over the Channel. I guess the night fighters were following us home, as they often did, fuel permitting. On our way up to base from the south coast I'm afraid I gave the crew a bit of a scare. While unloading the guns in the front turret, due to the fire and safe mechanism being frozen up, I let off a short burst inadvertently. Everyone was yelling at once, 'What's that? Where is it?' I might say it took quite a while for everyone to compose themselves again and, as you can guess, I was not the most popular man in the crew. What a relief it was to again be flying over Lincoln cathedral and hear Mike calling base, 'Hello Black Swan, this is Pilgrim "B-Beetham", permission to land?'

Back in debriefing we heard the full story of the squadron's effort. Out of the twenty aircraft from No. 50 Sqn on the operation 'Y-York' swerved on take-off ripping off her undercarriage delaying the rest of the squadron for forty minutes; 'L-London' pranged on return at RAF Winthorpe, went through two hedges finally standing on its nose, and three of our Lancasters failed to return. This was the worst night for No. 50 Sqn.

It was, indeed, a bad night for No. 50 Sqn. The first squadron aircraft was R5546, captained by Flight Sergeant D. G. Gray, which was shot down *en route* to the target. Gray baled out and survived to be taken as a prisoner of war, as did two other members of his crew but, unfortunately, his other four crew members were all killed, Sergeants J. Grant, D. Maughan, F. B. Patey and H. A. Wright are all buried in the Rheinberg War Cemetery. The second was EE174, captained by Flight Sergeant G. A. Waugh, shot down near Nuremberg.

Waugh and four of his crew managed to bale out and were taken as prisoners of war but two of his crew were killed, Pilot Officer D. L. Sehlin and Sergeant D. A. Chaston are both buried in the Darnbach War Cemetery. The third was LM394, which was captained by Flight Lieutenant M. U. Robinson, one of the flight commanders. His crew had an extra member on board that night and all eight were killed, Flight Lieutenant M. U. Robinson, Flying Officer T. W. Lavery, Flight Sergeants J. M. Mooney and V. A. Sanderson, and Sergeants J. B. D'Arcy, A. Horsfeld, A. R. Morgan and R. H. F. Ogbourne are all buried in Hanover War Cemetery.

For Bomber Command the Nuremberg raid was disastrous and effectively brought to an end, for the time being at least, the massed attacks against major cities, it would be some time before these tactics were employed again. With the nights becoming shorter, and preparations for the Allied invasion of Europe gathering momentum, the bombing offensive against German cities was effectively over and Harris turned his attention elsewhere. It had been a hard few months for both squadrons at Skellingthorpe. Between November 1943 and March 1944, No. 50 Sqn had lost ninety killed on operations and No. 61 Sqn had lost 129. Many more were either wounded or baled out over occupied territory and were taken as prisoners of war. Sadly, these losses at Skellingthorpe during the winter of 1943/4 can only be assumed to be typical of the losses across the many other airfields of Bomber Command at that time.

CHAPTER TEN

A Change of Emphasis

During the early months of 1944 it was clear to Harris and his senior commanders that the plan for the forthcoming Allied invasion of Europe would initially involve a massive campaign of air operations and, thereafter, would involve direct air support for the forces on the ground. Following the long and strenuous bombing campaign against Berlin and other major cities, it had become increasingly apparent that the war in Europe would only finally end with the defeat of German forces on the ground.

Although operational control of Bomber Command was not formally transferred to the Supreme Headquarters Allied Expeditionary Force (SHAEF) until 14 April 1944, Harris switched the emphasis from German cities to targets in occupied Europe immediately after the Nuremberg raid. This change in tactics was to support the overall aim of depleting German forces and to disrupt and destroy rail communications, particularly those affecting the movement towards the planned invasion lodgement area. The planned invasion of Europe was now less than ten weeks away and during the coming months there would be attacks against armament and ammunition factories and depots, railway marshalling yards and German troop concentrations, radar stations and coastal batteries, plus several more deception raids.

Because of the tactical difficulties of destroying precise targets by night, Bomber Command would also continue to attack industrial targets in Germany. Furthermore, the

161

Luftwaffe's night-fighter force was now operating at its peak in effectiveness. Aircraft production had been rationalized by reducing the number of aircraft types and airframe production had been dispersed out of the twenty-seven main manufacturing complexes into well over 200 small factories distributed throughout Germany and its occupied territories. There was a similar dispersal of aero-engine production, which meant that the industry overall was far less vulnerable to air attack than previously.

It was against this background that Les and crew found themselves as part of a small force of 145 aircraft from No. 5 Group on their way to bomb an aircraft factory at Toulouse on the evening of 5 April. With the exception of one aircraft, it was an all-Lancaster effort with the crews being taken from various main force squadrons. The only aircraft not a Lancaster was a Mosquito flown by Wing Commander Leonard Cheshire, who was then the commanding officer of No. 617 Sqn.

Leonard Cheshire needs little introduction as he was undoubtedly one of the most famous pilots who served with Bomber Command during the Second World War. At the age of just twenty-five years old he had been the youngest group captain in the RAF, but had reverted to the rank of wing commander to take command of No. 617 Sqn. At that time he had been awarded the Distinguished Service Order (DSO) and two bars, and the DFC. For some time he had demanded a smaller and faster aircraft for target marking and he eventually got his way. The Mosquito had been supplied to him for the purpose of carrying out low-level target marking and the raid on Toulouse was the first time that these tactics were employed. Cheshire successfully dropped his markers during his low pass over the target and these were followed up by more markers dropped from two Lancasters of his squadron. These tactics led to the raid being a total success and the factory was totally destroyed. Furthermore, this raid had proved that No. 5 Group now had a target-marking capability. Harris informed the group's commander, Air

Vice-Marshal Ralph Cochrane, that No. 5 Group was now considered to be an independent force and could operate as such using its own aircraft to mark rather than having to make use of the PFF. Leonard Cheshire went on to complete 100 operational sorties just a few months later, most of which had been flown against some of the toughest targets in Europe, and was awarded the Victoria Cross to add to his impressive decorations.

Whilst 5 April might have been a significant day, in terms of tactics, for No. 5 Group, it was an even more significant day for Pilot Officer Les Bartlett. His daughter, Diane, was born before he took off on the operation, so it is hardly surprising that his diary makes no reference to the raid but there is a brief note that marks the birth of his daughter.

Wednesday 5 April

Toulouse – No report from me.

Although my daughter, Diane, was born on 5 April, having been briefed for the Toulouse operation, my forty-eight hours compassionate leave did not commence until we returned to base.

Les returned home to spend valuable time with Margaret and Diane. Once again, for a few days at least, the war was forgotten. Les was actually granted more than the forty-eight hours referred to in his diary and he missed the crew's next operational sortie, which was flown against Aachen on the night of 11/12 April. However, he returned the next day and joined the crew in a training affiliation sortie with a Mosquito.

His next operation was flown against the railway marshalling yards at Juvisy, Paris, on 18/19 April. Again, with 202 Lancasters and four Mosquitoes from No. 5 Group, plus three Mosquitoes of No. 8 Group, the force was relatively small by previous standards. The night was typical of Bomber Command's tactics at the time. Whilst there were still occasions when a maximum effort would be launched against a single target, quite often Harris would split his assets against several similar targets. On this night, for example, Bomber Command launched a total of 850 sorties against four different railway marshalling yards. In addition to the 209 aircraft taking part in the raid against Juvisy, there were similar concentrated attacks against the railway yards at Rouen (289 aircraft), the marshalling yards and associated railway buildings at Noisy-le-Sec (181 aircraft) and the railway yards at Tergnier (171 aircraft). In addition, Bomber Command carried out mine-laying operations in the Baltic and off the coast of Denmark (a further 168 aircraft), and a further 100-plus sorties of minor operations against Berlin, Osnabruck and Le Mans, plus various radio counter-measure (RCM) sorties and Serrate patrols (Serrate was a British radar device designed to detect German night fighter transmissions). The total effort for the night was 1,125 sorties, which set a new record for Bomber Command; a total of just fourteen aircraft were lost (just over 1 per cent of all aircraft despatched).

These concentrated raids against targets in France brought a new challenge to the bomb aimer and his crew. In order to minimize the risk of casualties amongst the local French civilians, the crews were instructed only to release their bombs if absolutely certain that the target had been correctly identified and the aiming point was visible. The Juvisy raid was considered a success and, at four hours and twenty-five minutes this was the shortest operational sortie of Les's tour.

Tuesday 18 April – Rail Marshalling Yards, Juvisy, Paris

In order to make it difficult for the Germans to get their Panzer units to the Normandy coast (Panzers were transported by rail) it was decided to do as much damage as possible to the French marshalling yards. At briefing it was emphasized that in order not to kill French civilians, unless we could identify our aiming points we should return with our bombs. We obeyed orders and bombed successfully.

The bombing offensive, in terms of total Bomber Command sorties flown, had now reached another level. The record number of sorties flown on the night of 18/19 April was surpassed just two nights later when 1,155 were flown on the night of 20/21 April; again the effort was spread across a number of targets. Unsurprisingly, Les and the crew were once again involved, as was just about every available crew within the Command. Whilst the squadrons of Nos 1, 3 and 6 Groups were involved in the main effort against Cologne, No. 5 Group squadrons were despatched against the marshalling yards at La Chapelle just to the north of Paris. The raid again employed the low-level marking technique of No. 617 Sqn and the main force was spilt into two. Each force was given its own half of the target area to attack and the times on target were separated by one hour.

Thursday 20 April – La Chapelle Rail Marshalling Yards, Paris

We in 50 Sqn were proud to have been chosen to do this operation with 617 Sqn (the Dambusters) and three squadrons of Pathfinders. The same success at Juvisy was repeated at La Chapelle. On this occasion warnings were given at briefing about being careful with our bombs. No losses from the squadron.

There was a pattern developing; a maximum effort every two nights, with only a very minor effort on the night in between. No. 5 Group was now operating completely independently. Therefore, it was all-out effort again two nights later, on 22/23 April, when Bomber Command despatched a further 1,116 operational sorties. Again No. 5 Group essentially operated alone with a raid against Brunswick whilst the remaining groups, totalling 600 aircraft, were sent on the main effort against Düsseldorf. The No. 5 Group raid involved more than 250 aircraft and the low-level marking tactics were again employed, the first occasion when these tactics were used against a German city. The Brunswick raid, however, was not a success. Whilst it appeared that the low-level marking was accurate, a layer of cloud and poor communications on the night led to bombing becoming scattered. Clearly, there was nothing of note to be recorded, or else Les's mind was elsewhere:

Saturday 22 April – Brunswick (My 25th Operation)

No report from me. No aircraft lost from No. 50 Sqn.

Two nights later, there was another maximum effort with another 1,160 sorties flown but the Beetham crew were not involved. They were, however, back on operations two nights later when Bomber Command again despatched more than 1,000 sorties. Whilst the other groups went to Essen, more than 200 aircraft of No. 5 Group went to Schweinfurt. If the previous raid against Brunswick was assessed as 'not successful', then the raid against Schweinfurt can only be described as 'a failure'. During the transit the crews found the wind to be much stronger than forecast and this delayed the main force's time over the target. Also, for once, the low-level marking was not accurate and most bombs fell outside Schweinfurt. German night fighters also scored considerable success and twenty-one of the group's Lancasters were lost, nearly 10 per cent of those that took part in the raid. At just under nine hours duration, it was indeed a long night.

Wednesday 26 April – Schweinfurt (Our 26th Operation)

Operations came as expected this morning and we proceeded to do our NFT going for a change to the north of base and had a look at Doncaster. I did a little map reading just to 'keep my hand in' and Reg took Frank's place and took us back to base. He did not meet with much success at first but after many such hints as, 'I won't say where we are Reg, but I'm waving to Ena' (his girlfriend), we finally made it back to Lincoln. P/O Johnnie Blott has now finished his time with us but flew as passenger. After landing we took a few photographs then made for the mess to have lunch. The afternoon was spent lazily, writing letters and some of the late 'nighters' had a nap. Briefing time was 1715 hrs so we had tea first then went to the briefing. The target was Schweinfurt again.

It was rather a long trip but not a very difficult place, light flak eighty, heavy flak also about eighty and fifty searchlights. We were also getting cover from the main force, which were attacking Essen but this didn't turn out as expected as we became 'Joes' for them as they ended up losing far fewer aircraft than us. Take-off was at 2115 hrs and it was a real stage show, being broad daylight and a cloudless sky. Crowds of bods and many WAAFs becoming individually excited as their boyfriend's aircraft came round to turn on to the runway. I clearly remember seeing Joyce (Jock's popsie) waving and blowing him kisses, so futile against the slip-stream of a Lancaster!

As we roared down the runway and became airborne I got a further glimpse of crowds lining the Doddington Road end of the runway, civvies this time, they didn't realize what a dangerous spot they were standing in. If a kite should swerve off the runway or fail to become airborne, as is sometimes the case, they usually pile up and catch fire resulting in the bombs going up due to the heat. NO WAY would I stand there!

Having taken off a few minutes late due to the queue, we immediately got on course and settled down. I went down to my bombing compartment and proceeded to check the layout etc. – parachute on my left; rip cord on top; dinghy on my right; maps in the right order; guns loaded and cocked; gunsight switched on, then took things easy and put the usual amount of lanolin on my face to prevent the oxygen mask from chafing my chin.

At last we reached the Channel and darkness fell. The French coast soon became visible (only just) and as we neared it a few flashes in mid-air were observed, plus aircraft going down on fire. As no flak or tracer was seen I maintain it was due to aircraft crashing into one another in mid-air which caused the disaster. That is about the worst thing that can happen to you because you get no warning or time to jump. I'd rather be shot down any day! Things were fairly quiet south of Paris but got very lively as we approached Strasbourg. There were fighter Very flares all over the place and combats could be seen too. Around here I saw six aircraft go down in as many minutes. To make matters worse we got off track and when negotiating a turn on to a new course found ourselves in the thick of Karlsruhe's flak. For about a quarter of an hour they banged away at us but we weaved our way through it and we came within sight of the target.

As we got to the target the illuminating flares were going down and it looked a wonderful sight, as bright as day. We ran up and through the target as ordered to do, and then did a slow orbit. About halfway round we received a radio order to bomb, the target markers being OK. It took about three minutes to turn in and get on to our bombing run. Then I gave the order, 'Bomb doors open', and almost immediately, 'Bombs going.' Frank started giving me the time in seconds over the intercom and at thirty-two seconds our photoflash exploded simultaneously with the camera operating, and our job was complete. The target by this time was a sea of flashes and explosions; we certainly did a good prang. I later found out that we had the honour of being the only crew who brought back a photograph of the actual aiming point in the whole squadron. Beetham and his crew did it again!

While on our way out of the target area and lit up by the glare of raging fires I saw a sight that is rarely equalled. A Ju88 night fighter closed in with a Lancaster and opened fire. With his first burst the Lancaster caught fire but its gunners gave round for round immediately, and in no time the fighter was in flames. Both aircraft were by this time going down fast, yet 'Jerry' hung on grimly to the Lancasters tail, firing to his last round. The Lancaster gunners kept blazing away until the Lancaster was out of control and they could no longer get the Ju88 in their sights. Such an exhibition of bravery, dash and courage is rarely equalled, particularly among the *Luftwaffe*. If they cannot catch a bomber napping and have a very one-sided fight they will not 'play'. However, I am very much afraid neither our boys nor the enemy escaped to tell that story. They stuck to their guns until it was too late.

Our journey back was not very eventful. Apart from some evasive action to shake off a fighter and another that came head-on and was gone in a flash, we did not see anything worthy of mention. Skirting Paris, we saw the results of an attack, which had taken place a few hours earlier. Great sheets of flame were shooting skywards and looked terrific, although we must have been 30 to 40 miles away. As we neared the French coast, dawn showed signs of breaking but we did not relax our constant watch. It's such a shame to be shot down over the Channel after successfully cheating the enemy over his own territory. At last over good old England again we removed our oxygen masks and had a welcome cup of coffee. Now it was really light and we began to natter about the good pranging we gave Schweinfurt and it finished with the usual 'Beetham's crew does it again!' We're too modest, that's our trouble!

Back at base in the circuit were dozens of kites and they were not all 'playing the game'. Two rotten types, from No. 61 Sqn of course, cut a corner off the circuit and dived in front of us calling up control for permission to land as they did so. That meant we had to go back up to 2,100ft, instead of getting 'pancake'. We didn't care as we were back safely, so why worry. Three more trips like that and we are successfully through our tour – here's to them! No losses from 50 Sqn.

The crew's next sortie was flown on the night of 28/29 April against an explosive factory at St Medard-en-Jalles near Bordeaux. The crew were joined for this raid by Sergeant Kendrick who flew as rear gunner. The raid was again an all-No. 5 Group effort but consisted of just eighty-eight Lancasters and four Mosquitoes. Although some of the first bombers were able to identify the target area and bomb, by the time that Les's crew arrived the bombing had caused a number of fires in the surrounding area, which made identification of the target all but impossible. In such circumstances crews were ordered not to bomb and all aircraft returned safely.

Friday 28 April – St Medard-en-Jalles (27th Operation)

No losses. Brought our bomb load back as instructed.

Because of the importance of the factory, the bombers returned to bomb it the following night. For this attack it was decided to send a slightly smaller force of sixty-eight Lancasters, but again the Beetham crew were involved. This time Les was able to release their bomb load and the attack proved successful.

Saturday 29 April – St Medard-en-Jalles (28th Operation)

This time I could identify the target and bombed it. No losses.

Les had now completed twenty-eight operations and there was a strong light beginning to shine at the end of what had seemed to be an extremely long tunnel. As he had missed the Aachen raid on the night of 11/12 April, due to returning home on compassionate leave for the birth of his daughter, Diane, he now had just one last operational sortie to go; the end was now definitely in sight. However, it was no time to be complacent, as too many crews had failed to return from their last operational sortie.

It can only be assumed that the time spent waiting for a last operational sortie was somewhat nervy; a bit like in a game of cricket when a batsman is on ninety-nine not out and about to make his maiden century. Weather was a major factor in determining how long a crew had to wait; weather was, indeed, a major factor in determining how long a tour of operations lasted. Some crews waiting to complete their tour during winter would have to wait several days. Les noticed that their operational sorties were now coming more quickly as a result of improved weather and an increase in the operational tempo within No. 5 Group. He had flown seven operational sorties in April, the same number as he had managed in the two previous months. This meant that the Beetham crew did not have to wait long and their final operation was just two nights later; the target was a factory in Toulouse.

The contrast between his first operation, against Berlin at the heart of the Reich on the night of 22/23 November 1943, and now his last against Toulouse, a city in the south of France, is a fine example of how the emphasis of Bomber Command's offensive during the winter of 1943/4 had changed. At the end of the Berlin offensive about 70 per cent of the Command's effort had been against targets in Germany. As preparations for the forthcoming Allied invasion of Europe entered the final stages, Bomber Command widened its effort to include the German communication system, railway networks and factories. During April 1944 less than half the total number of bombs dropped were against targets in Germany and during May over 75 per cent of sorties were against targets in France and other occupied territories. Six of Les's last eight operational sorties were flown against targets in France.

The comparison between the raid against Berlin on 22/23 November 1943 and the one against Toulouse on 1/2 May 1944 not only provides an interesting contrast in the target but also demonstrates the general change in the way that Bomber Command's groups were now operating and the fewer losses suffered. During the raid against Berlin Les and his crew were one of 764 aircraft taking part in the only major operation of the night, which involved the various groups within Bomber Command. A total of twenty-six aircraft were lost on the raid (3.4 per cent). Although this figure was lower than the average at the time, twenty-six aircraft still represents a considerable loss. Including minor operations, Bomber Command managed a total of 802 sorties that night. In comparison, it flew a total of 801 sorties on the night of 1/2 May 1944. The difference was, however, that the Command attacked six different targets and lost just nine aircraft (1.1 per cent). In addition to Toulouse, No. 5 Group mounted a second but smaller raid against Tours; No. 6 Group went to St Ghislain; No. 4 Group went to Malines; No. 3 Group went to Chambly, and No. 1 Group went to Lyons. Aircraft from No. 8 Group were used in support of the larger efforts against St Ghislain, Malines and Chambly.

And so the Beetham crew prepared for their final operational sortie on 1 May; at times it had seemed to Les as though the day would never come. They had been to Toulouse just a few weeks before, so the target area was known to Les. It was now just a matter of getting airborne and hoping that their trusted Lancaster, LL744, remained serviceable. Coded VN-B, affectionately known to the crew as 'B-Beetham' rather than the more correct 'B-Baker', the crew flew this aircraft on twenty operations. More importantly, they had flown it consecutively on their last eighteen operations, and to be forced into any change of aircraft at such a late stage would be bad luck. The superstition of having a lucky aircraft was strong amongst many Bomber

Command crews and there were many examples of a crew being lost having changed aircraft for reasons such as their 'lucky' one being unserviceable on the day. However, Les need not have worried, LL744 did not let them down. Although Toulouse was a round-trip of seven and a half hours, the sortie did not present any problems; bombs were dropped, the factory was hit and all the 131 Lancasters returned safely. When the Beetham crew touched down back at Skellingthorpe there was relief all round; their tour of operations was over.

Monday 1 May – Toulouse

No report from me. Too tired.

THIS WAS OUR LAST OPERATION. GLAD IT'S ALL OVER!

CHAPTER ELEVEN

Life Would Never Be The Same Again

Having completed a tour of operations, having survived the Battle of Berlin, having survived the disastrous Nuremberg raid along with many other deep excursions into Germany and occupied France, the obvious question for Les when he awoke on the morning of 2 May 1944 was 'Where does life go from here?' Going home on leave to see his wife Margaret and baby daughter Diane, still less than a month old, was an obvious priority but it was not to be quite as straightforward as that. It was, after all, wartime and there was still a job to be done with No. 50 Sqn before the crew was posted to go their separate ways.

The following day they took their replacement crew on a familiarization sortie and check flight in the trusted LL744 'VN-B', no longer to be 'B-Beetham' but to revert to 'B-Baker'. The trip lasted just forty minutes and it was to be Les's last with the squadron. That night, the target was a military camp near the French village of Mailly-le-Camp but it would not involve the Beetham crew. They had done their bit. They were all lucky not to be involved, as losses that night were high. Forty-two Lancasters failed to return from the raid (11.6 per cent of the force), including five aircraft from No. 50 Sqn. Twenty-five of the squadron's aircrew that had woken up at Skellingthorpe that morning did not live to see the next.

As for Lancaster LL744, the trusted chariot of the Beetham

crew, it did not see the month out, it was lost less than three weeks later when it was one of thirteen Lancasters that failed to return from Brunswick on the night of 22/23 May; six of the crew were killed. It was a tragic reminder that there was still a long way to go before the bombing war was over and the losses suffered on the Mailly raid left a feeling of depression hanging over Skellingthorpe as Les left the base. He had said his goodbyes to his crew colleagues as they went off to their various instructional tours, which was quite normal at the end of a tour of operations. Mike Beetham was posted as an instructor to No. 5 Lancaster Finishing School, Jock Higgins moved to Brackley to become an OTU instructor and Reg Payne was posted to Silverstone to train wireless operators. As with any other Bomber Command crew that survived an operational tour, the bond formed between the young men would remain with them for the rest of their lives.

Having spent two weeks at home on what he called 'survivor's leave' Les returned to Lincolnshire for his next posting as a staff bomb aimer instructor back on No. 1654 HCU at Wigsley. It was June 1944. He now had time to reflect on what had happened in the nine months since he had first arrived at Wigsley as a student bomb aimer. It seemed like years ago, rather than months. In such a short period he had experienced such high points, the birth of his daughter, successfully completing his tour of operations, the award of the DFM and his subsequent commission as an officer. Yet, during the same nine months, he had experienced some extremely low points, such as the loss of so many friends, none of whom were more missed than his two crew members Fred Ball and Don Moore. His life would simply never be the same again.

Not only had so much happened to Les, there had also been a major development in the war with the Allied invasion of Europe. The break-out from the Normandy beaches meant that Bomber Command could not, for the time being at least, resume a full-scale offensive against Germany. The Lancasters were instead involved in attacks against coastal batteries, lines of communications, railways and enemy troop positions. There were also raids against the Germans' V-weapon sites in the Pas de Calais area and Bomber Command was able to resume daylight operations, the first for over a year, as the bombers now enjoyed the luxury of fighter escort for the shorter-range missions. Things had changed but there was still much to do and new crews needed to be trained. It would be almost another year before the war in Europe would come to an end.

Les's main task during the summer of 1944 was to help train crews for two Australian squadrons, Nos 463 and 467, based at Waddington. His return to Wigsley also provided him with the opportunity to renew his friendship with the Dixon family at North Scarle. Although he had not lost touch whilst at Skellingthorpe, the time spent on operations had meant that he had found little time to socialize. Now back at Wigsley he did not waste much time before calling to inform them that he had safely got through his tour of operations. Naturally they were delighted and he was invited for Sunday lunch the first time that he was free. Fortunately for Les, the family who lived opposite the Dixons had a spare room and a few days later he was joined by Margaret and baby Diane so that they could spend a few days together in North Scarle. And so began a lasting friendship between the Bartletts and the Dixons, as well as many other local families in the Lincolnshire village of North Scarle.

Now that Les had completed his operational tour, he was able to focus on 'ordinary life' once more. He needed a car so that he could more easily make the journey between Wigsley and his family at Billingham when leave came around. A good friend offered him a 1932 Hillman Minx, which had been off the road since the outbreak of war, for £20. Although the car could not have been described as a 'classic', and there were no spares to be found, for Les it was just what he needed. The problem he now faced was how to get petrol, which was rationed. He soon found out that he was entitled to a petrol ration provided that his wife lived nearby. He found a good bed and breakfast in Richmond Road, Lincoln, and once he had an address he was able to go to the station headquarters and register the 'arrival' of his family. With the formalities over, Les soon had a petrol ration book in his hand with, he recalls, an allowance of about 2 gallons per month.

Of course, 2 gallons of petrol a month would not go far and Les soon learned about the various 'scams' around the base. One was either to bribe the aircraft refuelling tanker drivers or to siphon fuel from the aircraft. The aircraft fuel was then mixed with tractor paraffin, which was freely available from the farms given the right contacts, and the mixture worked a treat. The car went 'like a bomb, the only problem was that the exhaust fumes were something else!'

The contacts that Les had managed to build up in the local area almost got him into trouble one day whilst he was travelling north to County Durham to see his family. The route he took was northwards straight up the Great North Road (the A1), which took him through the centre of Doncaster. On one occasion he was approaching the centre when he came across several police dealing with an accident. Not only was Les in his Minx 'aircraft fuel and paraffin convertible' but he was also carrying half a pig and eggs for his family, which he had managed to pick up from a farmer friend at North Scarle – well over the limit of fresh meat that could be transported at any one time. Rather than run the risk of passing through the police at the accident, he decided to take an alternative route. When he eventually arrived at Billingham, the family were delighted with the fresh meat and there was plenty for everyone. What was not eaten was exchanged for a pair of shoes for Margaret. That was how life went on during the war.

For the remainder of 1944, Les taught precision bombing to student crews on the Stirling and Lancaster. Most training sorties were flown by day and lasted typically between two and three hours, although there were some longer and others shorter. Instructing consisted of much classroom teaching, as well as airborne instruction, with a comfortable balance compared to what life had been like on operations. He would never know how many of his students would survive the war; all he and his fellow instructors could do was to prepare them as well as he and his colleagues had been trained just a year before.

In March 1945 Les went on a course at No. 1 Empire Air Armament School at nearby RAF Manby. It involved a mix of high- and low-level flying in the Wellington, which to Les seemed a bit of a step-down, having been more used to the Lancaster. He returned to Wigsley just before the end of the war in May.

On 6 June 1945 he flew what was known by Bomber Command crews as a 'Cook's Tour', which was named after the English travel agent Thomas Cook. These tours gave the crews the chance to fly around various cities in Europe to observe for themselves the results of the long and concentrated bombing campaign. Les recalls that there was a strong desire amongst many Bomber Command personnel to see what was left of Germany. It also provided an opportunity to take some of the ground crew flying as a way of thanking them for all their efforts during the war.

For his 'Cook's Tour' Les flew with Flight Lieutenant Innis, a fellow instructor at Wigsley, in Lancaster 'JF-O-Oboe'. With twelve ground crew on board, they first flew to over Brussels and then set off on their 'tour', which took them over Maastricht–Aachen–Duren–Cologne–Düsseldorf–Duisburg–Dortmund–Essen–Hamm–Eindhoven–Arnhem–Amsterdam and then back to base. Understandably, the trip left lasting memories for all those who witnessed it. At a height of just 500ft, they were able to observe in detail the scenes of devastation. In places there seemed to be nothing left, just piles of rubble. By the time they returned to Wigsley they had been airborne for more than six and a half hours.

Les enjoyed his time at Wigsley. Most of the staff and students were Australians and he has good memories of their character, joviality and generosity, as well as their extreme professionalism. Although the war in Europe was over, there was talk of a Tiger Force being formed from Bomber Command crews to go out to the Far East, where the war against Japan was still ongoing. However, for Les this was only talk and nothing was to materialize. Instead, he returned to the Empire Air Armament School at Manby to attend No. 108 Bombing Leaders' Course. This involved more high- and low-level bombing on the Wellington and lasted eight weeks.

For Les, 31 July 1945 was one of the proudest days of his life. Just a few days before he had received an important-looking envelope from St James's Palace marked 'immediate'. He guessed straight away what it was and eagerly opened it to find that he was invited to attend Buckingham Palace the following Tuesday to receive his Distinguished Flying Medal from the King. There was little time to prepare and, before he knew it, he and Margaret were entering Buckingham Palace. Although the investiture was short, the memory was ever-lasting.

The end of the war meant that the focus for Bomber Command, and the RAF in general, was very much on a mass demobilization of its wartime personnel and a reduction in its equipment and bases. The future of Wigsley was therefore as a satellite airfield for nearby Swinderby. Another airfield facing a similar future was Skellingthorpe, which also became a satellite airfield for Swinderby. The long-term future of these two airfields, which had become so important to Les, was uncertain; in the end neither survived long into the 1950s.

As a result of the general draw-down, Les was posted to No. 1660 HCU at Swinderby at the end of August 1945 with his old unit, No. 1654 HCU, moving out to Woolfox Lodge soon after. Swinderby opened its gates to the general public on 15 September, the fifth anniversary of the Battle of Britain, for the first post-war 'RAF at Home Day'; thousands of local civilians attended to see the flying and static aircraft on display.

The following month Les again went back to Berlin by Lancaster, but this time he went to visit the city. Post-war politics saw Berlin divided into four sectors by the Allies, one each for the US, the UK, France and the Soviet Union. The

UK's sector consisted of the boroughs of Tiergarten, Charlottenburg, Wilmersdorf and Spandau. With each of the four Allied powers keen to maintain a visible presence in and out of the city, there were several RAF flights to and from Berlin in the months immediately following the end of the war. To the crews these were known as 'flag-waving' trips and, as always, Les was keen to go. He got his chance when one of the staff pilots at Swinderby, Flight Lieutenant Harrison, chose him as one of his crew. On 20 October they took off in Lancaster 'TV-U-Uncle' and first flew to Tibenham in Norfolk for customs clearance before going on to Berlin. Having detoured over Brunswick and then over Magdeburg to view both cities from the air, they landed at Gatow in the south-western borough of Spandau. Compared to the long trips to Berlin and back that he had undertaken during his tour of operations, it was a short transit at just over two and a half hours.

The airfield at Gatow had been constructed in the mid-1930s and was originally used by the *Luftwaffe* as a staff and technical college, *Luftkriegsschule II*, along the same lines as the RAF College at Cranwell. The airfield was captured by Russian troops during late April 1945. Following Germany's surrender, the main Allied leaders met in the Berlin suburb of Potsdam during late July and early August to determine the division of post-war Germany. As a result, the four occupation zones were set up and the airfield at Gatow was relinquished by the Soviet forces in exchange for the one at Staaken-Dallgow. Initially known as Intermediate Landing Place No. 19, the airfield then became RAF Gatow on 19 August 1945.

RAF Gatow remained one of the RAF's most important overseas air bases for the next half century. Eventually, following the reunification of Germany after a long and tense Cold War, the British ceded control of the airfield back to Germany in September 1994, soon after which it was closed to air traffic.

On arriving at Gatow, Les and his colleagues were met by

the army garrison commander. They were immediately asked if they were carrying any weapons. They were not and were promptly issued with a Russian pistol and a sock full of ammunition. For the next couple of days Les and his colleagues were billeted in a block of flats just outside the airfield. Meals were taken in the pre-war Yugoslav Embassy, which had been converted into an officers' mess. They were waited on by the staff and enjoyed good food, along with the contents of the cellar full of wines and champagne.

The lifestyle enjoyed by Les during his brief visit to Berlin was in total contrast to what the local inhabitants of the city were suffering at the time. During the final days of the war, the Allied decision to halt British and American forces at the River Elbe had left Berlin open and the city finally capitulated to the Russian army on 2 May 1945. Living conditions for Berliners in the months following the end of the war were basic to say the least, with many living in underground basements and cellars. The locals had not enjoyed the period of Russian occupation and Les suddenly found that being from the West seemed to entitle him to life like royalty. Before leaving Swinderby he had been advised by crews from previous visits to take as many luxury items as possible, such as coffee and soap. He soon found out that these items were more important to the locals and he managed to exchange his coffee for a three-stone diamond ring for Margaret.

Les was determined to make the most of his couple of days in Berlin and decided to see as much of the city as possible. An army sergeant who had got to know the area well agreed to show him around. They first visited the Chancellery and then the *Führerbunker* where Hitler had spent his final days before ending his life. He then visited what was left of one of Berlin's railway stations. All that was left were the platforms; the walls, roof and ancillary buildings had all gone. There were groups of people sitting on the platforms with what was left of their personal belongings as if they were waiting for a train. There were no trains and, for the time being, the railway station was their home.

Having flown ten of his operations against Berlin, witnessing such scenes understandably made Les feel partly responsible for the destruction and devastation caused. By the end of the war about a third of Berlin had been totally destroyed as a result of Allied air attacks and ground fighting. In some parts of the city, particularly in the central areas, destruction of the buildings and infrastructure was almost total. Les momentarily shared his thoughts with his guide and then moved on to the Tiergarten where he saw one of the large reinforced concrete flak towers, which had been built as part of the city's defences. Les climbed to the top. On the roof was a battery of 108mm anti-aircraft guns. He was surprised to find that the flak tower had completely survived despite the devastated surrounding area.

Les's brief two-day visit was soon over and he was on his way back to Tibenham to clear customs once again. With a headwind the flight took three hours but this proved valuable time for the crew as they all had something to hide. They knew the Lancaster aircraft very well and they had little trouble concealing their bounty. Les dismantled the sighting head of his bomb sight and hid the diamond ring inside. Once on the ground, they completed the necessary paperwork and were soon on their way back to Swinderby. It had been a brief visit but the memories would be everlasting.

Les's return to Berlin was sooner than he might have expected and it came about just a few weeks later when he heard that his old squadron was organizing another flag-waving visit to the city. No. 50 Sqn had left Skellingthorpe at the end of the war and had moved temporarily to nearby Sturgate before moving to Waddington in January 1946. It was during the move to Waddington that Les picked up word that the squadron was sending an aircraft on a flag-waving trip to Berlin. Les was now a flight lieutenant and in the officers' mess he met up with the pilot, Flight Lieutenant Lloyd, who agreed to take Les on the trip. So on 15 January 1946 Les found himself on the way to Berlin once more. Again they flew via Tibenham to clear customs and three hours later

Les was at Gatow, again armed with 'exchangeables' such as cigarettes, coffee beans and soap.

During his second visit back to the city Les noticed quite a difference, even in the space of less than two months. The centre of Berlin seemed much tidier as rubble had been piled high on the sides of the roads, which made it easier to get around. He visited the Kaiser Wilhelm Church and what was left of the Reichstag. The goods he took out were exchanged for an old decorated plate of a traditional German warrior and a beautiful water set consisting of a jug and six glasses. Whilst the plate and jug have lasted to this day, the glasses did not last very long as Les dropped the box they were in whilst getting out of the truck before boarding the aircraft for the return trip!

As usual, the crew all had excess alcohol on board and two dozen bottles of champagne somewhat amazingly survived the journey back to Swinderby via the inner engine nacelles, Flight Lieutenant Lloyd having made two of his softest landings ever! Les's cargo hardly put him very high up in the league of 'what could be brought back from Germany in a Lancaster'; many much larger items found their way back to England via the bomb bay!

The opportunity to go back to Berlin on these 'flag-waving' trips left lasting memories, although it would be more than half a century before Les would return to the 'big city' once more.

Les's second daughter, Christine, was born on 21 January 1946, just three days after he returned from his second flag-waving visit to Berlin. Soon after, he received news that he was to be demobilized from the RAF and was offered a posting near his home. He found out there was an assistant adjutant's post at Thornaby at Billingham, where his wife Margaret and two young daughters were still living with her parents, and Les was soon on his way. Arriving back at Thornaby brought fond memories flooding back. Sixteen years had passed since the days when, as a young boy, he used to cycle 6 miles to the airfield just to stand at the perimeter fence to watch the Westland Wapitis of the Auxiliary Air Force. Now he was back.

He moved in with his family at Billingham, and for the first time, he and Margaret were able to enjoy what might be regarded as a 'normal' married life; albeit that they were still living with Margaret's parents. The journey to Thornaby was much quicker in his car than the cycle ride he used to endure. Life seemed normal once more and suddenly the war seemed like years ago. Les reported to the Adjutant and was immediately made most welcome. His duties were to be general administration with particular responsibility for entertainment and welfare. At the time the airfield was in Coastal Command and the resident Warwicks of No. 280 Sqn had the task of air-sea rescue.

With his responsibility for entertainments, Les felt in his element. There was a large drill hall with a reasonable stage and his first task was to organize a weekly dance. Right from the start it proved to be a success and word soon got around the local area. Les had become a good friend of Jim Gardener, a local band leader from Stockton, and the event got bigger and bigger. Although the local civilians had to pay admission, Les laid on courtesy buses to nearby Stockton. The evening started at 8 p.m. with Les playing the Ted Heath Orchestra's 'Skyliner' on the public announcement system to get the crowd in the mood. Then the curtains were pulled back as the band took over from the record. The Thornaby weekly dance nights certainly left a lasting impression on Les as well as others who were there.

If entertainment proved to be the high point of his time at Thornaby, the welfare aspect of his job was just the opposite. He found himself increasingly having to deal with personal and domestic problems for which he had received no specialist training whatsoever; nonetheless, he did the best he could.

Les knew that on leaving the service he would require reliable transport. He had managed to acquire a replacement engine for his 1933 Ford 8 car, courtesy of the education officer at Thornaby, who was running rehabilitation classes for the benefit of airmen approaching demobilization and wishing to learn a trade. At the back of the hangar was a Boulton Paul turret, which had been used by the air gunner training unit, mounted on a structure powered by a Ford 8 engine. The engine had hardly been used and it was, indeed, too good an opportunity to miss. However, as there was no way it could be removed from the station without being noticed, the education officer agreed that his car mechanic classes would strip it down so that Les could then get the parts into his car and off the station. Les had expected the engine to be stripped down into three main components; the cylinder head, the cylinder block and the sump. Unfortunately, the class had stripped down every item possible and he was left with the task of rebuilding the engine himself. Fortunately, his father-in-law had a garage and Les spent the following weeks putting the engine back together again. Then, with a little help from his friends, he managed to take out his old engine and replace it with his 'new' rebuilt one. The engine worked like a dream and it meant that Les could now, once again, make the long journey down to Southampton to visit his parents.

Les had fond memories of his final posting in the RAF but it was time to put the war behind him and to move on; it was only natural that, having qualified as a pharmacist in 1940, there was a profession waiting for him and he should return to pharmacy. He applied for various appointments with national drug companies that appeared in the *Pharmaceutical Journal*. He was soon invited to attend an interview at the headquarters of Evans Medical Supplies at Speke near Liverpool. There was no problem getting there; Les simply arranged for an Avro Anson to take him from Thornaby to Hawarden and this is the last entry in his RAF flying log book.

The interview was a success and Les was offered a position as a company representative covering the North and East Ridings of Yorkshire, along the Yorkshire coast down to the River Humber and inland to the Yorkshire Moors and Dales.

He had loved his time in the RAF but this was just ideal and the sweat and tears spent on rebuilding the engine for his car suddenly seemed worthwhile.

Les was officially demobbed from the RAF on 14 May 1946. He travelled from Thornaby to the demobilization centre at Wembley where he was issued with a suit, which he could choose from a very limited selection, a pair of shoes, an overcoat and a trilby hat. He was given six weeks' 'demob' leave and, after a short stay with his parents, decided to take his family on holiday to Jersey. Unfortunately, tickets from Southampton to Jersey were hard to come by as there were only seven per flight available for passengers. After two days of trying he was still unsuccessful and so he dropped a hint that he had served in the RAF during the war. He was quietly advised by one of the airport staff to turn up at 9 a.m. the following day in his uniform. It worked wonders. The combination of his flight lieutenant's rank and his DFM ribbon meant that he and his family were on board the Dragon Rapide the following day and in Jersey by lunch time.

On his return from his holiday in Jersey, Les started his new career. Space precludes us looking at his long life since 1946 in any detail. He enjoyed seven years working for Evans Medical Supplies before he saw an opportunity to establish a new pharmacy in Billingham. He maintained close contact with his family in Southampton and decided to sell up and move south in 1960. Having moved to Bursledon on the edge of Southampton, he opened a new pharmacy and also bought an established pharmacy in nearby Woolston. In 1969 he and his family moved to Hamble and spent many happy years there until Margaret sadly died in February 1998.

Les has always maintained a fascination for aircraft and has recorded all of his post-war flights, whether going on holiday or simply taking a joy ride in the local area. One of the most notable flights was his trip on Concorde in November 1985, which came about following a visit to the International Air Tattoo at Fairford in Gloucestershire. Having purchased a copy of the local newspaper, Les entered a competition where he needed to identify various parts of an aircraft. Of course, for him, it was easy but he was amazed when an envelope arrived at home the following week informing him that he had won the competition and his prize was a flight in Concorde! On 2 November 1985, with Captain Brian Walpole at the controls, he was aboard Concorde heading out over the Channel. During a champagne-fuelled flight of one and a half hours, he flew at Mach 2 over the Atlantic. During the flight he was delighted to be invited to the flight deck where the three crew members signed his RAF flying log book. It was, indeed, an unforgettable flight.

Another notable memory was a return flight from New York, following a short Christmas shopping trip in December 2002. On boarding the United Airlines Boeing 777 for his flight home Les asked the purser to bring him the name of the captain and the aircraft registration so that he could enter the details of the flight in his RAF wartime log book. A few minutes later the purser returned and explained that Captain Gallagher would be pleased to see him. Whilst the co-pilot continued with the pre-flight checks the captain was keen to learn all about Les's wartime experiences. Although the two men could have talked for hours it was time to get going and the captain instructed the purser to put Les into first class for the trip home. Needless to say, for Les the experience really was first class and he ended up falling asleep in total comfort; it certainly was a trip that he would never forget. On landing at Heathrow, the captain said goodbye, but keen to return the hospitality in some way, Les offered him a sight-seeing tour of parts of Hampshire should he ever have time during a stop-over and gave him his contact details. Two months later he got a phone call from Captain Gallagher during a stop-over to take him up on his offer. Needless to say Les was delighted.

Not surprisingly Les has never forgotten his wartime experiences or his close colleagues, in particular the other four surviving members of the original Beetham crew. In the same way that they all came together from different backgrounds, they all went their different ways at the end of the war. The rear gunner, Jock Higgins, was demobbed at the end of the war and joined the Palestine Police Force. He spent a few years in Israel before returning to his home in Glasgow. He then married Fay before moving to Canada during the 1950s. He made the journey from his home in Toronto back to Skellingthorpe in 1989 for the unveiling of the Nos 50 & 61 Squadrons Memorial. A keen golfer, Jock died in 1993 – on the golf course.

The navigator, Frank Swinyard, became a certified accountant. He joined the Merchant Seamen's War Memorial Society as Company Secretary and Accountant. The society had a convalescent home in Limpsfield Chart in Surrey and a 400 acre farm training centre for disabled seamen, known as Springbok Farm, at Alfold in Surrey. Married to Pam they lived in East Horsley, Surrey. In 1963 the society was reorganized and Frank became overall manager. Eighteen bungalows housed retired seamen and their families and the convalescent home had a purpose-built wing added to the main Victorian mansion in which potential farmers were housed. Frank devoted his life to making the venture a total success. During his time, more than 1,000 men and their families were helped to build new lives after becoming ill or suffering accidents whilst serving as seamen. On retiring in 1982 he and Pam first moved to Sussex and then to Highworth, Wiltshire, in 1991. By then his health was failing and he spent the last years of his life in hospital and a nursing home in Stratton St Margaret, Swindon.

The wireless operator, Reg Payne, was demobbed in August 1946 and worked in the engineering industry before he eventually retired. He now lives with his second wife, Freda, in Kettering. Reg has never forgotten his time in the RAF and has spent more than fifty years as a member of the Royal Air Force's Association and is president of his local branch.

The only member of the crew to remain in the post-war RAF was the pilot, Mike Beetham. His post-war career could be the subject of a book on its own as he went on to command at every level, eventually becoming Marshal of the Royal Air Force Sir Michael Beetham GCB CBE DFC AFC DL FRAeS. His appointments of note included: Officer Commanding No. 214 Sqn at Marham during the late 1950s, as one of the first V-bomber squadron commanders equipped with the Vickers Valiant B.1; Station Commander at RAF Khormaksar in Aden, the RAF's biggest overseas station, during the mid-1960s; Commandant of the RAF Staff College and then Commander-in-Chief RAF Germany and the Second Tactical Air Force during the early and mid-1970s; and five years as Chief of the Air Staff between 1977 and 1982.

Having begun his distinguished career in wartime, Sir Michael's forty-one years of full-time active service ended in conflict as a member of the Chiefs of Staff Committee during the Falklands War of 1982. He was then promoted to the rank of Marshal of the Royal Air Force, the highest possible rank that could be attained in the service. He later became Chairman of GEC Avionics. He has remained active in many roles and capacities ever since and amongst his many positions he holds the appointment of Honorary Air Commodore of No. 2620 Sqn, Royal Auxiliary Air Force Regiment and is President of the RAF Museum and the Bomber Command Association. Despite remaining a very busy man in his eighties, he always finds time to join up with his surviving crew members and colleagues at the annual reunion of the Nos 50 and 61 Squadrons Association, of which he is President, at the former site of RAF Skellingthorpe near Lincoln.

Today Les still lives in Hamble, near Southampton, and is now in his ninetieth year. He has many memories of his wartime experiences and his life since. He is also amazed at some of his chance meetings with locals whilst on holiday – examples of how small the world seems to him at times. One example was his conversation over a glass of wine with a local whilst on a caravan holiday in France during the early 1970s. It turned out that the Frenchman had been studying

dentistry in Paris during 1944 and had witnessed the RAF's
bombing of the rail marshalling yards at La Chapelle on 20
April, which had been Les's twenty-fourth operation.
Another was when Les met a German lady on a skiing
holiday in Yugoslavia during 1975. She had been just eight
years old and living in Leipzig during the winter of 1943/4.
She described in detail what life was like during the air raids
and what it was like spending night after night in the shelters;
Les had bombed Leipzig twice during the period. Then there
was another German lady who had been born in Frankfurt
during the same period and Les realized that her mother
would have been in the last stages of pregnancy during the
RAF's bombing.

Whilst Les has had sobering thoughts over the years of
what life must have been like on the receiving end of an air
raid, he also has many fond memories during recent years of
his gatherings with his wartime colleagues, as a member of the
Bomber Command Association, the Aircrew Association and
the Nos 50 and 61 Squadrons Association.

In 1986 he attended the Annual General Meeting of the Nos
50 and 61 Squadrons Association when the members first
discussed the possibility of erecting a memorial at the
Birchwood Leisure Centre, which was located on the site of
the former wartime airfield of RAF Skellingthorpe. As a result
a Memorial Committee was formed and Les volunteered to be
one of the six members.

For the following three years the Memorial Committee met
frequently in Lincoln to decide how to raise the £26,000
required, where the memorial would be located and its
design. The money was eventually raised and the wonderful
memorial built from Norwegian granite by Leake's Masonry
of Louth. On 3 June 1989 it was unveiled by Marshal of the
Royal Air Force Sir Michael Beetham, Les's wartime pilot. It
was an immensely proud moment, not only for Les and Sir
Michael but also for all those who attended.

The former site of RAF Skellingthorpe has long been
developed into a large residential housing estate and there

are few reminders of what happened during the Second World War. The memorial is still as impressive as ever. It stands proudly on the site where No. 50 Sqn and No. 61 Sqn once served and has taken on increasing importance as word of the brave men of both squadrons has been passed down amongst the local population.

In June every year the Association holds its annual reunion weekend on the former site of the airfield. During the weekend the wartime veterans are hosted by the local people of Skellingthorpe village and entertained by the young children of the Leslie Manser Primary School. The school is named after Flying Officer Leslie Manser VC, who was posthumously awarded the Victoria Cross whilst serving with No. 50 Sqn at Skellingthorpe, for his gallantry in saving the lives of his crew on the first Thousand Bomber raid to Cologne on the night of 30/31 May 1942. The close association between the wartime members of the squadrons and the local population is typical of the true admiration that the people of Lincolnshire have for Bomber Command. It is during the weekend's events that Les gets the chance to meet up with the two other surviving members of his wartime crew, Sir Michael Beetham and Reg Payne.

Amongst other recent memories, Les was honoured to be invited to Clarence House on 23 February 2000, when Her Majesty Queen Elizabeth the Queen Mother invited members of the Bomber Command Association to visit her at home. Les was one of the lucky ones and was delighted to be introduced to the Queen Mother by his former wartime pilot, Sir Michael Beetham. Although she would not have remembered Les, he was quick to point out that they had met once before when she stood alongside King George VI during the investiture when Les was decorated with the DFM in July 1945. As so often with such memorable events, it was soon all over and time to leave but this wonderful occasion will be everlasting for Les.

Soon after Les was given the chance to see the Queen Mother again, although this time he would not meet her in person. He was part of her 100th Birthday Parade on 19 July 2000 at Horse Guards Parade; it was yet another extremely proud moment for Les as he gave his best 'eyes left' during the march past.

In addition to his proud memories, Les has a personal reminder hung on his lounge wall of his wartime tour of operations. Throughout his training and his operational tour Les always flew with a white silk scarf, which he had bought before the war for wearing with his dinner jacket. He took it with him when he reported to the Air Crew Reception Centre in 1941; his only explanation is that he thought it might bring him luck. All through his training it went everywhere with him. Eventually, whilst waiting to go on his first operational sortie, he decided that he would get a bottle of ink and mark his scarf with the name of the target. He would wear the scarf on all his operational sorties and add the name of each target as he progressed through his tour. The rest of his crew were not particularly keen on this idea should they ever be shot down and captured. And so, in no uncertain terms, they made it clear that should this ever happen he would very much be on his own. Les refused to give in and, of course, this did not happen.

Fifty-six years after his last visit to the 'big city', Les visited Berlin on a British Legion Tour of Berlin, Colditz and Leipzig during October 2002. By then, the city had a population of some 3½ million and what Les saw was completely unrecognizable from what he had seen in January 1946. So much had happened to the city. The post-war division of Germany had placed Berlin in a somewhat unique position. It was half-controlled by the West, although it was deep in East Germany, and this made it a natural focal point throughout the Cold War. During 1948–9 there had been the year-long Soviet blockade of ground routes in and out of Berlin from the west in the hope of gaining complete control; this resulted in the Allies becoming involved in a massive logistical effort to supply the western sectors of the city through the Berlin Airlift. Eventually, the blockade was lifted and the Soviets again allowed ground access to West Berlin. Then there had been the June Uprising in 1953 when there was a general strike following action the previous day by construction workers in East Berlin demanding a reduction in work-quota increases. The general strike and protest marches turned into rioting, which spread throughout East Germany and was eventually suppressed by Soviet troops; more than 150 people were killed.

There then followed the biggest political statement made in post-war Berlin; the Berlin Wall. Construction of the wall began in 1961 as a response by the Communist East German government to prevent the massive numbers of East German citizens fleeing into West Berlin. The wall completely separated the eastern and western sectors of Berlin and the only possible way of passing from one side of the city to the other was through strictly controlled check points. During the Berlin Wall's existence it is believed there were about 5,000 successful escapes into West Berlin but nearly 200 people were killed attempting to reach what they believed to be a better life.

Berlin was the centre of much of the Cold War espionage activity as the US and Russia confronted each other. Gradually, over the following decades, the Iron Curtain weakened as Communism in Europe weakened and more and more people fled to the West through other East European countries. At the fortieth anniversary of the formation of East Germany in East Berlin in October 1989, Mikhail Gorbachev indicated that Russia would not support the hard-line East German regime. The East German leadership was in disarray and the following year Germany and Berlin were both reunited. By then the Berlin Wall had almost been completely demolished, with only small sections remaining. Finally, in 1991 Berlin once again became the capital of a unified Germany.

The city had become part of Les' life. A simple toy for his sixth birthday had first made him aware of it, but he could never have known how much a part of his life it was to become. He returned once more in August 2005, just before his eighty-eighth birthday. It was a short trip of just four days, although he managed to find the time to visit the graves of some of his colleagues who had been less fortunate than himself.

Les is now fast approaching his ninetieth birthday and he looks forward to the various reunions which he always attends. Those of us privileged to know him agree that he is a remarkable man and one of life's true survivors. His story has at last been told.

Bomber Command Order of Battle, November 1943

No. 1 Group

12 Sqn	Lancaster	Wickenby
100 Sqn	Lancaster	Grimsby
101 Sqn	Lancaster	Ludford Magna
103 Sqn	Lancaster	Elsham Wolds
166 Sqn	Lancaster	Kirmington
460 Sqn (RAAF)	Lancaster	Binbrook
550 Sqn	Lancaster	Grimsby/North Killingholme
576 Sqn	Lancaster	Elsham Wolds
625 Sqn	Lancaster	Kelstern
626 Sqn	Lancaster	Wickenby

No. 3 Group

15 Sqn	Stirling	Mildenhall
75 Sqn (RNZAF)	Stirling	Mepal
90 Sqn	Stirling	Wratting Common
115 Sqn	Lancaster	Little Snoring
149 Sqn	Stirling	Lakenheath
196 Sqn	Stirling	Witchford
199 Sqn	Stirling	Lakenheath
214 Sqn	Stirling	Chedburgh
218 Sqn	Stirling	Downham Market

514 Sqn	Lancaster	Foulsham
620 Sqn	Stirling	Chedburgh
622 Sqn	Stirling/Lancaster	Mildenhall
623 Sqn	Lancaster	Downham Market

No. 4 Group

10 Sqn	Halifax	Melbourne
51 Sqn	Halifax	Snaith
76 Sqn	Halifax	Holme-on-Spalding Moor
77 Sqn	Halifax	Elvington
78 Sqn	Halifax	Breighton
102Sqn	Halifax	Pocklington
158 Sqn	Halifax	Lissett
466 Sqn (RCAF)	Halifax	Leconfield
578 Sqn	Halifax	Burn
640 Sqn	Halifax	Leconfield

No. 5 Group

9 Sqn	Lancaster	Bardney
44 Sqn	Lancaster	Dunholme Lodge
49 Sqn	Lancaster	Fiskerton
50 Sqn	Lancaster	Skellingthorpe
57 Sqn	Lancaster	Scampton
61 Sqn	Lancaster	Skellingthorpe
106 Sqn	Lancaster	Syerston
207 Sqn	Lancaster	Langar
463 Sqn (RAAF)	Lancaster	Waddington
467 Sqn(RAAF)	Lancaster	Waddington
619 Sqn	Lancaster	Woodhall Spa
630 Sqn	Lancaster	East Kirkby

No. 6 Group

408 Sqn (RCAF)	Lancaster	Linton-on-Ouse
419 Sqn (RCAF)	Halifax	Middleton St George
420 Sqn (RCAF)	Halifax	Tholthorpe
424 Sqn (RCAF)	Halifax	Skipton-on-Swale
425 Sqn (RCAF)	Halifax	Tholthorpe
426 Sqn (RCAF)	Lancaster	Linton-on-Ouse
427 Sqn (RCAF)	Halifax	Leeming
428 Sqn (RCAF)	Halifax	Middleton St George
429 Sqn (RCAF)	Halifax	Leeming
431 Sqn (RCAF)	Halifax	Tholthorpe
432 Sqn (RCAF)	Lancaster	Skipton-on-Swale
433 Sqn (RCAF)	Halifax	Skipton-on-Swale
434 Sqn (RCAF)	Halifax	Tholthorpe

No. 8 Group

7 Sqn	Lancaster	Oakington
35 Sqn	Halifax	Graveley
83 Sqn	Lancaster	Wyton
97 Sqn	Lancaster	Bourne
139 Sqn	Mosquito	Wyton
156 Sqn	Lancaster	Warboys
405 Sqn (RCAF)	Halifax	Gransden Lodge
627 Sqn	Mosquito	Oakington
635 Sqn	Lancaster	Downham Market
692 Sqn	Mosquito	Graveley

Total: 68 squadrons

Major Bomber Command Raids on Berlin, November 1943 – March 1944

Note: Aircraft losses in brackets.
Raids that the Beetham crew flew on are shown in bold.

Date	Total A/C	Lancaster	Halifax	Stirling	Mosquito	Tonnage
Phase I						
18/19 Nov	444 (9)	440 (9)	–	–	4	1,594
22/23 Nov	**764 (26)**	**469 (11)**	**234 (10)**	**50 (5)**	**11**	**2,465**
23/24 Nov	**383 (20)**	**365 (20)**	**10**	–	**8**	**1,335**
26/27 Nov	**450 (28)**	**443 (28)**	–	–	**7**	**1,576**
2/3 Dec	458 (40)	425 (37)	15 (2)	–	18 (1)	1,686
Phase II						
16/17 Dec	493 (25)	483 (25)	–	–	10	1,815
23/24 Dec	379 (16)	364 (16)	–	–	8	1,288
29/30 Dec	**712 (20)**	**457 (11)**	**252 (9)**	–	**3**	**2,315**
1/2 Jan	**421 (28)**	**421 (28)**	–	–	–	**1,401**
2/3 Jan	383 (27)	362 (27)	9	–	12	1,116
Phase III						
20/21 Jan	**769 (35)**	**495 (13)**	**264 (22)**	–	**10**	**2,401**
27/28 Jan	**530 (33)**	**515 (33)**	–	–	**15**	**1,761**
28/29 Jan	**677 (46)**	**432 (20)**	**241 (26)**	–	**4**	**1,954**
30/31 Jan	534 (33)	440 (32)	82 (1)	–	12	1,961

Date	Total A/C	Lancaster	Halifax	Stirling	Mosquito	Tonnage
Phase IV						
15/16 Feb	**891 (43)**	**561 (26)**	**314 (17)**	–	**16**	**2,643**
24/25 Mar	**811 (72)**	**577 (44)**	**216 (28)**	–	**18**	**2,493**
TOTAL	9,099 (501)	7,249 (380)	1,644 (115)	50 (5)	156 (1)	29,804
Diversionary Raids						
21/22 Jan	**34 (1)**	**22 (1)**	–		**12**	**Div. Magdeburg**
19/20 Feb	15 (1)	–	–		15 (1)	Div. Leipzig

In addition there were several minor operations flown against Berlin, all of which were flown by Mosquitoes. These were on (number of sorties in brackets): 24/25 November (6), 25/26 November (3), 3/4 December (9), 4/5 January (13), 5/6 January (13), 10/11 January (10), 14/15 January (6), 1/2 February (12), 5/6 February (18), 10/11 February (21), 3/4 Mar (16), 4/5 March (15), 19/20 March (9) and 25/26 March (10). The only losses occurred on the night of 24/25 November (1 aircraft) and 1/2 February (1 aircraft).

Operational Sorties Flown by Les Bartlett

Op.	Date	Aircraft	Target	Flt Time	Remarks
1	19 Nov 43	DV217	Dinghy Search	4.05	
2	22/23 Nov 43	JA899	Berlin	7.15	
3	23/24 Nov 43	JA899	Berlin	7.45	Landed Wittering
4	26/27 Nov 43	DV376	Berlin	8.05	Div. Melbourne
5	3/4 Dec 43	DV376	Leipzig	7.50	Waddington–Wittering
6	20/21 Dec 43	ED588	Frankfurt	5.40	
7	29/30 Dec 43	LL744	Berlin	7.25	30lb bomb – wing
8	1/2 Jan 44	HK537	Berlin	8.15	
9	5/6 Jan 44	DV376	Stettin	8.40	
10	14/15 Jan 44	ED856	Brunswick	5.10	
11	20/21 Jan 44	LL744	Berlin	7.00	
12	21/22 Jan 44	LL744	Berlin	7.25	Div. for Magdeburg
13	27/28 Jan 44	LL744	Berlin	8.55	
14	28/29 Jan 44	LL744	Berlin	7.55	Damaged Ju–88
15	19/20 Feb 44	LL744	Leipzig	7.00	
16	25/26 Feb 44	LL744	Augsburg	8.00	Ret on 3 engines
17	1/2 Mar 44	LL744	Stuttgart	8.10	
18	9/10 Mar 44	LL744	Marignane	8.55	Bombed 10,000ft
19	24/25 Mar 44	LL744	Berlin	7.20	Div. Fiskerton
20	26/27 Mar 44	LL744	Essen	5.05	

Op.	Date	Aircraft	Target	Flt Time	Remarks
21	30/31 Mar 44	LL744	Nuremberg	7.45	
22	5/6 Apr 44	LL744	Toulouse	6.55	
23	18/19 Apr 44	LL744	Juvisy	4.25	
24	20/21 Apr 44	LL744	La Chapelle	4.30	
25	22/23 Apr 44	LL744	Brunswick	6.00	
26	26/27 Apr 44	LL744	Schweinfurt	8.50	
27	28/29 Apr 44	LL744	St Medard	8.00	
28	29/30 Apr 44	LL744	St Medard	7.20	
29	1/2 May 44	LL744	Toulouse	7.35	

Note: Les missed the crew's operation to Aachen on 11/12 April 1944 due to being on compassionate leave following the birth of his daughter.

Index